# The SEVENTH LEVEL

# The SEVENTH LEVEL

## Taking Your Faith to the Level of Perfection

by

Lloyd W. Blount

Unless otherwise noted, all Scripture quotations are from the Authorized King James Version of the Bible. All biblical word definitions are taken from www.esword.com.



Cover Design by Eric Pipes, Envision Graphics
eric@envisiongraphics.net

Published by:

McDougal & Associates
18896 Greenwell Springs Road
Greenwell Springs, LA 70739
www.ThePublishedWord.com

McDougal & Associates is dedicated to the spreading of the Gospel of Jesus Christ to as many people as possible in the shortest time possible.

ISBN 978-1-940461-26-7

Printed on demand in the US, the UK and Australia
For Worldwide Distribution

# Dedication

I dedicate this book to the memory of my father, Milton C. Blount. I was just a small boy when he endured his greatest trial of faith and persevered until victory came. His faith has inspired me to hold on in the darkest moments of life, with the assurance that my trial, too, has an end, and that I, too, will achieve complete and perfect victory.

# Acknowledgments

I want to thank my dear brother, Harold McDougal, for encouraging me to put this message into a book. After hearing me preach it for the very first time, he said to me, "Pastor, this message has to go into a book so that others can be blessed by it." I never forgot those words. They have become reality only because he worked the material into its present form and then kept after me until I made the final adjustments on it.

Thanks to my lovely wife Regina for her inspiration and support and for believing in me.

I am indebted to Faith Sawyer who patiently listened to my preaching CDs and transcribed from them the material for this book and to Eric Pipes, who sought God until he had just the right cover design. Thank you both.

# Contents

# Introduction

Many fine Christian believers are wondering why they are not getting answers to their prayers and why they are suffering something they feel sure they should not be suffering as a child of God. "Is something wrong with my faith?" they wonder. They have done everything they know to do to lay claim to a certain biblical promise, and yet it seems to elude them. "What's wrong with me?" their soul cries out.

If you are among those who are questioning God in this way, questioning your faith, or even questioning your spiritual experience, I want to assure you that nothing is wrong with you, and nothing is wrong with your faith. God loves you, and you love Him, and that means you are His child and heir to all of His great promises.

So how can we explain the fact that you are being so severely tested? There is a process that is necessary to your ultimate spiritual maturity, and many of the negative things that happen to you on a daily basis are simply part of that process, part of God's order of things.

These are things that the God who loves you intensely allows to happen because His desire is that your faith be perfected. He wants you to take your faith from one level to the next ... until you have reached *The Seventh Level*. How is that possible? What is required of you? And what exactly do I mean by *the seventh level*? Stay with me, and we'll discover the answer to these and many other great mysteries together in the pages of this book.

*Lloyd W. Blount*
*Hammond, Louisiana*

## Chapter 1

# Possessing a Now Faith

> *Now faith is the substance of things hoped for, the evidence of things not seen.* Hebrews 11:1

The writer of Hebrews declares: *"Now faith is."* What does that mean? It means that now faith just simply and positively is. Is what? It is *"the substance of things hoped for,"* and it also is *"the evidence of things not seen."* That thought stretches us. It gets on our nerves. It scratches against the carnal part of us. It disturbs our flesh. It sets our nerves on edge. And when you get your nerves set on edge, it affects all those around you. All of this comes because what we are reaching for is *"not [yet] seen."*

*Now faith* is the kind of faith that is current. It's up to date. It's for the here and now. It will help you through the trials of this very day.

*Now faith* is *"the substance of things hoped for."* It's good to have hope, isn't it? Hope paints a picture, and it's a very beautiful, colorful panoramic view. It's there somewhere out there in the atmosphere.

But faith then goes further than hope. Faith reaches out and brings that hoped-for thing into reality. Faith causes that hoped-for thing to actually become *"evidence."*

This evidence is not in your mind, it's not in your body, and it's certainly not in your emotions. It is in your spirit. Faith, then, is spiritual evidence.

Spiritual evidence is substance, but it is the evidence of things *"not seen,"* and that often causes us a problem. We war with things not seen. Personally I've always warred with things that I could not see. There is something about our nature that causes us to want to see a thing. We have to see it. We just have to see it. We simply have to see it.

Then, after we have seen a thing, we want to go further. We want to touch it with our own hands. If we can't see it and we can't touch it, we have difficulty laying hold of it. But *now faith* is the substance of things hoped for, and it is the evidence of things not yet seen. That's the kind of faith God requires.

Now, at this point, I need to ask an important question: what do you do when there is nothing, no substance and no evidence? What do *you* do? Well, we've already read what God has to say about it. He speaks of a spirit world in which we can have faith in our hearts for something, although right now nothing seems to exist. What you're dealing with is nothing, and what do you do when there is nothing?

Is there a known strategy for dealing with nothing? Is there a certain way you should go about it, when dealing with nothing? Let me clarify where I'm going with all of this.

When we speak of nothing, we are speaking of nothing in the realm of the natural. I'm not suggesting that there is nothing in the realm of the Spirit. Oh, there is. It exists in that realm. We just can't see it yet, so we have to lay hold of it by faith and pull it into our everyday world.

Let's look at the sixth verse of that same chapter of Hebrews. It says:

> *But without faith it is impossible to please him: for he that cometh to God must believe that he is, and that he is a rewarder of them that diligently seek him.*
>
> Hebrews 11:6

What is the writer saying here? Where there is no faith, no biblical, scriptural, God-kind, God-given Word-type faith, we cannot please Him. Why would that be? It's because of the fact that He is so almighty and so powerful, because of the fact that He was, He is, and He will be.

That which is is, and that which is had to be, or was. That may not seem be the best English, but it helps me see things from God's perspective. That which is is God. He is the God who always was, the God who always is, and the God who always shall be. He is all three in one, all at the same time. Oh, wow!

To please Him, we must first believe that He is and then that He is (at the very same time) a rewarder of them that diligently seek Him. How do we diligently go after God and all that He has for us? We're dealing with faith here, and we're dealing with the need to bring that faith to another level, even to the seventh level (which we will soon understand).

This has nothing to do with the anointing. That's a whole separate issue. There are levels of anointing, but here I'm talking about levels of faith. Your faith can be lifted today to a new level in God, and we'll soon see why His goal for you is that your faith rise to the seventh level.

The anointed writer added:

> *Looking unto Jesus the author and finisher of our faith; who for the joy that was set before him endured the cross, despising the shame, and is set down at the right hand of the throne of God.*
>
> Hebrews 12:2

*"Looking unto Jesus ..."* This is a call for us to consider Him. *Look,* as it is used here, means "to gaze or stare, set your eyes upon, focus your eyes upon, glue your eyes to." It also means "to take heed." So to consider Him means to put everything else totally out

of sight and out of mind and concentrate on Him. *"Looking unto"* who? *"Looking unto Jesus."*

This verse describes Jesus as *"the author and finisher of our faith."* Whose faith is it? It's ours, mine and yours. You have a faith, and it is that faith which will determine your future. You will not be judged by God's faith. No, He is the Author and Finisher of *your* faith. It is what *you* believe and declare that will determine your destiny.

If you declare, "I will never be broke again," and you believe it in your heart and act upon it, that will be your portion. Take hold of it today.

I must be looking unto Jesus, for He is the Author and the Finisher of my individual faith, whatever level it happens to be on at the moment. Jesus is the *Author* of it, meaning that He is the Originator of my faith.

This word *Finisher* is very powerful. It means that He is also the Perfecter of my faith. That indicates that my faith can grow and rise to new levels with His help.

I started this chapter by stating that God desires for your faith to be perfected, and that can be accomplished because Jesus is the Author and Finisher of it, meaning that He is the Originator and the Perfecter of it. Now, this does not mean that He does everything for you, and you have no responsibility in the matter. No! He doesn't shave me in the morning, and He doesn't brush my teeth for me either.

I hate to shave and wish the Lord Jesus would do it for me every day, but He's doesn't do that, and He won't do it, so I can't expect it. I have to shave myself, and I have to get myself dressed in the morning, among many other things. He is our Source, and He enables us, equips us, and graces us to do His will, but we are the ones who must actually do it. He doesn't do it for us.

One of the definitions for *grace* is "God's divine ability inside of us for us." It is given to you, but then you have to do something with it. It is God's divine ability in you, but you have to activate it. You must do His will, but God will grace you to enable you to do it. So, when the Scriptures say that Jesus is the Author and Finisher of our faith they mean that He, through His Word, creates and initiates faith in us, and then He enables us to go on to perfect it.

How does this faith come to us? The Scriptures are very clear on this point:

> *So then faith cometh by hearing, and hearing by the word of God.* Romans 10:17

Faith comes to us when a Spirit, or *rhema,* word proceeds from the mouth of one of God's anointed servants, and we hear it. Jesus is the Author of it. He has inspired that word and only uses the mouth of His servants among us to deliver it.

So that's how faith begins. But how is faith perfected? Since Jesus is the Perfecter of it, it is by and through His daily dealings with us (through His ways and plans) that our faith is perfected. Jesus gives us plans. He gives us strategies for dealing with life's situations, and as we follow Him faithfully, our faith rises to ever new heights.

I have a responsibility in all of this. He gives me the strategies, often through the lessons of the Bible, but I must put them into action. God provides the plans and the strategies, or the ways and means, but I am responsible to carry them out. This is how I get my faith perfected and rise to a new level in God.

Now, in the next chapter, let's discover what I mean by this phrase *The Seventh Level*.

## Chapter 2

# "Go Again Seven Times"

*And Elijah said unto Ahab, Get thee up, eat and drink; for there is a sound of abundance of rain. So Ahab went up to eat and to drink.*
*And Elijah went up to the top of Carmel; and he cast himself down upon the earth, and put his face between his knees, and said to his servant, Go up now, look toward the sea.*
*And he went up, and looked, and said, There is nothing.*
*And he said, Go again seven times.*

1 Kings 18:41-43

*"And Elijah said unto Ahab, Get thee up, eat and drink; for there is a sound of abundance of rain. So Ahab went up to eat and to drink."* I can imagine that Ahab moved pretty fast. Infidel that he was, he believed the words of this prophet.

*"And Elijah went up to the top of Carmel; and he cast himself down upon the earth, and put his face between*

*his knees."* In other words, Elijah got into a humble, worshipful, and believing position, but it was also a relaxing and restful position, and that's important too. Faith is not always a terrible struggle. Relax and learn to trust God.

Elijah then turned to his servant and told him to go up and look for rain. The man obeyed, but returned to say, *"There is nothing."* That was definitely not what the prophet wanted to hear. I don't like to deal with nothing, and I'm sure you don't either. What a nasty word: NOTHING!

But this is a word that we all need to deal with on a daily basis, and it is a word we must not be afraid of. Nothing does not mean the end for us, as believers in Christ. We should know how to deal with Nothing, for the Master of Nothing lives within us.

The fact that Elijah sent the man to look demonstrated some level of faith on his part. He was expecting the man to see something. He told the man exactly where to look and what to look for. But when he had looked exactly where he was told to look, there was nothing. This must have been emotionally distressing for the prophet.

The fact that the servant went as he was told and looked as he was told demonstrated a certain level of faith on his part. His master had said there would be rain in a certain direction, so he had looked in that direction, expecting to see rain, but there was nothing.

This must have been emotionally distressing for the servant as well.

Then, on top of that disappointment, he had to go back and report that there was nothing. "I looked where you told me to look, where you were expecting me to see something, but there was nothing." It should have been there, but it was not. This must have left both men deeply frustrated.

But this was not the end of the matter. When there is nothing, remember that it's not over yet. That's not the end of things. *"Look again,"* Elijah commanded, and he kept sending the man to look, and the man kept going and looking ... until he eventually saw what he had expected to see all along:

> *And it came to pass at the seventh time, that he said, Behold, there ariseth a little cloud out of the sea, like a man's hand.*
>
> *And he said, Go up, say unto Ahab, Prepare thy chariot, and get thee down that the rain stop thee not.*
>
> *And it came to pass in the mean while, that the heaven was black with clouds and wind, and there was a great rain. And Ahab rode, and went to Jezreel. And the hand of the LORD was on Elijah; and he girded up his loins, and ran before Ahab to the entrance of Jezreel.* 1 Kings 18:44-46

The desired and expected result came, but it took seven times of going for it to happen. What does this mean to us on a practical level? It means that we must bring our faith up another notch and another until it has been perfected, until it has reached the seventh level.

All believers have a certain level of faith. Some, after hearing one powerful word from God, believe that they have arrived. Their faith seems to be bursting at the seams, but the Lord is not impressed. That's just the first level of faith, and He will not be satisfied until their faith has been perfected.

Jesus was not impressed with the faith of those around Him, sometimes even that of His own disciples:

> *And yet I say unto you, That even Solomon in all his glory was not arrayed like one of these. Wherefore, if God so clothe the grass of the field, which to day is, and to morrow is cast into the oven, shall he not much more clothe you, O* YE OF LITTLE FAITH? *Therefore take no thought, saying, What shall we eat? or, What shall we drink? or, Wherewithal shall we be clothed?* Matthew 6:29-31

> *And his disciples came to him, and awoke him, saying, Lord, save us: we perish. And he saith unto*

*them, Why are ye fearful, O YE OF LITTLE FAITH? Then he arose, and rebuked the winds and the sea; and there was a great calm. But the men marvelled, saying, What manner of man is this, that even the winds and the sea obey him!*

Matthew 8:25-27

*And when his disciples were come to the other side, they had forgotten to take bread. Then Jesus said unto them, Take heed and beware of the leaven of the Pharisees and of the Sadducees. And they reasoned among themselves, saying, It is because we have taken no bread. Which when Jesus perceived, he said unto them, O YE OF LITTLE FAITH, why reason ye among yourselves, because ye have brought no bread? Do ye not yet understand, neither remember the five loaves of the five thousand, and how many baskets ye took up? Neither the seven loaves of the four thousand, and how many baskets ye took up? How is it that ye do not understand that I spake it not to you concerning bread, that ye should beware of the leaven of the Pharisees and of the Sadducees? Then understood they how that he bade them not beware of the leaven of bread, but of the doctrine of the Pharisees and of the Sadducees.*

Matthew 16:5-12

I suppose little faith was better than no faith at all, but Jesus was not impressed with it. These men and women may have had a measure of faith, a certain level of faith, but it was not enough for their current situation, and that's what counts. These were not faithless people, and yet Jesus rebuked them. And who wants to be rebuked by Jesus? I know I don't.

So what do you do when there is nothing? You go again, and you keep going — even if it takes seven times. If you go and there is nothing, it must mean that God is up to something. You haven't understood it all yet, but He knows what He's doing. So just go again. If you keep going, He will eventually bring forth something out of nothing for you.

This phrase *"go again"* means "to turn back, to go back, to start over." That's where we make our mistake. We tend to stay right where we are. You have to go back and keep going back until you find what you're looking for. Start over and keep starting over until your answer comes.

*"Go again"* also means "to return to the starting point," and that's a problem for most of us. We are so full of pride that we don't want anyone to know that we've made a big loud confession and then discovered that there was nothing. And we hate to be seen going back to look again. We hate others knowing that our faith is not absolutely perfect. "They will see me and know there is nothing." Oh, how we dread that!

Pride torments us with the thought of anyone seeing us going back to the starting line, but with real faith, we know our limitations and don't mind getting up and doing it all over again. We don't mind returning to the starting point, going back to prayer, going back to worship, praising again, giving again, believing again, confessing again, and then doing it all over again and again ... until the breakthrough comes. Going back is not our idea of progress, but in this case, we're going back to the Well, going back to our Source, going back to the place of seeking. *"Go again."*

Going again means returning to the place where God once gave us instructions. Instead of trying to rewrite the instructions yourself, get back to the Source and let Him show you how to do it like He wants it done.

We must remember that God does not deal with us all in the same way. He knows us individually and deals with us on our particular level. He knows our backgrounds, what formed us, and why we do what we do. So He tailors every instruction to suit the individual person. He has also stated that when we know more, then more is expected of us. You wouldn't expect the same from a child of two as you would from a son who is twenty, so why should God? Trust Him to know your testing needs.

"Go again," and if it takes seven times, then go seven times. Don't stop going until you have obtained the victory.

But why did Elijah say to go seven times? Why not five times? Why not ten times? What is special about the number seven? In the Scriptures, seven represents completion. It means fullness, actually referring to an indefinite number. God made the number seven this way. He determined a number that would signify to us any number at all.

To go seven times signifies order and preciseness, and our God is a God of order and preciseness. His work, His doings, and His ways are very orderly, and His instructions are very precise. This is always important to remember. There is a purpose behind everything that God says and everything He does. There is a purpose for His particular order. So, *"go again,"* that your faith may rise to another level and be perfected.

Do you really expect God to go easy on you just because you've had a bad day, a bad week, a bad month, or a bad year? No matter what you have been hearing others say, God will hold you accountable for your actions, even if you've been having a hard time of it. We have known many great men and women of faith who, at times, had it very bad. It seemed that everything was going wrong for them, and then they got even "wronger." But these men and women did not use this as an excuse to slack up and let down on their faith. The result was that their faith matured and carried them through. They persevered because they knew that God would hold them accountable if they didn't. Therefore they could not do otherwise.

We are responsible to God for what we do, and we are responsible to bring our faith to the next level and the next ... until it reaches the seventh level, that level of perfection. Why is this so important? There is always a purpose in God's order. In the case of Elijah, the word had already gone out: *"There is a sound of the abundance of rain."* When God drops something into our spirit, there is an eternal purpose for it, and we must see it through to the desired end. *"Go again"* until your victory is complete. Go on the *The Seventh Level*.

## Chapter 3

# Discovering the Significance of Your Nothings

*And said to his servant, Go up now, look toward the sea. And he went up, and looked, and said, There is nothing.*
*And he said, Go again seven times.*

1 Kings 18:43

The fact that there is, or seems to be, nothing never controls or affects God. No, *Nothing* does not control Him; He controls *Nothing*. That may sound crazy to some, but think about it. Understand what I'm saying. I am not saying, as would be the usual use of these words, that God is not in control of anything. In this case, we're not talking about the word *nothing* in its usual context. We're talking about a state of being, a condition, a place of existence (or non-existence, if you like). This state of being is called Nothing, and God controls that state. God controls the place called Nothing, and so impossibilities do not exist there.

Let's try to picture this place called Nothing. It's dark, it's empty, and it's void, and yet impossibility cannot and does not exist in that place, for the God of the Universe lives and works and manifests Himself inside and outside of Nothing.

In fact, since God created everything that exists, we can conclude that God created Nothing. Now, why would He do that? Jesus stated very strongly:

> *I am come that they might have life, and that they might have it more abundantly.* John 10:10

If God's purpose on the earth was to bring life, why would He create Nothing? Perhaps He did it just so He could use that Nothing to bring your faith to perfection. Because you often have to deal with Nothing, that empty and fruitless place where nothing is visible to the naked eye, you are forced to work at building your faith to overcome. So Nothing is actually a blessing to you, not a curse.

What exactly does this word *nothing,* as used here, mean? When the servant said, *"There is nothing,"* what was he saying? *Nothing* here means "no speck, blot, or spot." Nothing! What a great word! God created Nothing so that your faith could be perfected, and so you must deal with the nothingness of life on a daily basis, and you should be happy about that fact.

Those Nothing areas in your life that you are so distressed about … God created them for your spiritual benefit. He chose to present you with them so that you could overcome and rise to perfection in Him.

So Nothing is created by God, and God creates Nothing. But understand that for God, Nothing is something. God's Nothing really is something.

How can Nothing be something? If God created Nothing, then it has a good purpose. God's Nothing is something. It is something real. We say it's Nothing, but wait. Did you know that Nothing really is something?

Nothing is a place that is specifically designed by God for your life. It's a place that was designed to look like nothing, but it really is something. And do you know why you are dealing with it? You may not understand it for a while, but if you remain faithful, one day you *will* understand. God will bring forth something out of your Nothing.

Anything you deal with in life is something. In this case, the something you are dealing with just happens to be Nothing. This Nothing is something created by God, and since He is everywhere, He is right there in that dark, unfruitful place. He's just waiting to be discovered, and He will be discovered by faith.

As you deal with your Nothing, suddenly your blessing will come. This process may seem sporadic and unpredictable, but it was carefully planned and purposed all along. In the very same way, your place called Nothing was also part of God's plan and purpose, so that your faith could be fully tested and perfected. So, instead of feeling bad about the Nothing in your life, learn to thank God for it. Say, "Thank You, Lord, for my Nothing. What a beautiful place! Although I don't see anything in my Nothing right now, I know it's there because You purposed it for my perfection. Help me to deal with it in a way that is pleasing to You." Then *"go again"* and keep going until the cloud appears.

*"Go again"* necessarily means to go back and face your Nothing, and who wants to do that? But we must. It is out of that Nothing that will come the something God has determined for your life.

Human nature being what it is, I can imagine that this servant might have complained. "You're sending me back to look into the face of Nothing again?"

"Yes, go again."

We all have to deal with Nothing in certain areas of our lives. Your Nothing may be different from my Nothing, but it's still Nothing. Except that now we know that Nothing is not really nothing; it's really something. So don't despise your Nothings. There's a reason for them. Don't despise your empty places. They have a higher purpose.

Both Elijah and his servant experienced six times of Nothing, and each time they were forced to return to the starting point and look again. The prophet said *"seven times,"* and he meant *"seven times."* So it was not enough to make the excuse, "But I've gone three times already, and there is still nothing." Three times is not enough. We have to keep reaching higher.

The fourth time there was nothing, the fifth time there was nothing, and the sixth time there was still nothing. This could have led one or both of them to conclude that the result would be the same with each subsequent trip, and if they had believed that, they would have been tempted to quit trying.

Somehow I believe that this servant knew that he was on a journey, and his own faith was being tested. If not, he could have said he went and looked even if he hadn't. He, too, had a certain level of faith. He knew that his master was a man of God, and he knew that when he said, *"Go seven times,"* there was a reason for it. I am convinced that when this servant went the seventh time, he went with a renewed expectancy. He *would* see something this time, and, of course, he did.

Each time we try and fail, it only gets harder. Going the sixth time was not easier, but harder than the fifth. With each failed attempt, the enemy must have put on more pressure, mocking and scorning the effort, and vowing that no amount of trips would bring any different result. He is a master at making a mountain out of mole hills.

With each trip, the Nothing became more Nothing. It became more dark and more fruitless. In that Nothing space was even more nothing. There was nothing inside of the Nothing. By the sixth time, the Nothing had grown in nothingness.

But the man of God had said, *"Go seven times."* Every test eventually comes to an end and hopefully a glorious one. The trial of your faith will seem to stretch out so long until you wonder if it will ever end. Then, when you have reached the seventh level, something will suddenly break loose, and all because your faith has matured through facing the prescribed trial.

Every single one of the seven trips was necessary. You can't take a shortcut. You can't wiggle your way out of the test. God's order is precise, and if He says, *"Go seven times,"* then it's one, two, three, four, five, six, and seven, and you can't leave one of the steps out, or you just might have to start all over again.

If, in the process, you quit, then you lose. If you quit, you're out. When you are in doubt, you're out. You can't rewrite the order of God. He desires that your faith be perfected, and since the number seven means completion, you must complete God's requirements, however long it takes and whatever it costs. You have no choice in the matter. The Almighty God designs our tests, and He always knows best. So do whatever you need to do to get to the seventh level, and until you have reached that level, you really haven't accomplished much.

Was the servant tired when he trudged back for the seventh time? Perhaps, but the important thing is that he went, and this time he saw something different. Instead of the Nothing he had been looking at for so long, there was now Something.

This Something the servant saw was not very big. In fact, it was really rather small:

> *And it came to pass at the seventh time, that he said, Behold, there ariseth a little cloud out of the sea, like a man's hand.* 1 Kings 18:44

It doesn't all come at once. Once we have obtained a perfected faith, then God wants to see if we will hold on to it. Faith is a most valuable commodity. We must cherish and nurture it, and we must do whatever is necessary to perfect it. That's when we will begin to have a truly effective testimony. Please don't stop at level five. Press on to perfection.

You might feel that you have struggled and struggled, and you are tired of the struggle, but don't give up. The victory is only another level away. Don't stop until you have reached that seventh level, no matter what it takes. Keep praising, keep worshipping, keep giving, keep doing, stay faithful and loyal to God. Your time of blessing is nearing. *"Go again."* Go to *The Seventh Level.*

## Chapter 4

# Joshua's Rise to the Seventh Level

*Now Jericho was straitly shut up because of the children of Israel: none went out, and none came in. And the* Lord *said unto Joshua, See, I have given into thine hand Jericho, and the king thereof, and the mighty men of valour. And ye shall compass the city, all ye men of war, and go round about the city once. Thus shalt thou do six days.*

*And seven priests shall bear before the ark seven trumpets of rams' horns: and the seventh day ye shall compass the city seven times, and the priests shall blow with the trumpets. And it shall come to pass, that when they make a long blast with the ram's horn, and when ye hear the sound of the trumpet, all the people shall shout with a great shout; and the wall of the city shall fall down flat, and the people shall ascend up every man straight before him.* Joshua 6:1-5

Is this principle of the seventh level really biblical? Oh, yes, there are many examples of it in the Scriptures. Here's another one. In Joshua's time, when he and his people were ordered to march around the walls of Jericho, you will remember that it took them seven days and seven times on the seventh day.

They marched around the first day, as ordered, but nothing happened. The next day the result was the same. Nothing had changed. After three days, four days, five days, and six days, THERE WAS NOTHING. But Joshua didn't give up, and his followers didn't either. Instead, on the seventh day, they blew trumpets and shouted, and it was in that moment that the change came. Their faith had matured, and so God said, "Now watch what will happen with these walls."

What happened at Jericho is one of the strangest phenomena ever recorded. Instead of falling in or out, the walls of the city actually sunk down into the ground, forming a sort of walkway, and the children of Israel easily crossed over and took possession of the city. It happened after they had fulfilled their seven-day march and their seventh time around on the seventh day. Their faith (and the accompanying obedience) had reached the seventh level. They had fulfilled God's order.

Just because we speak in tongues we sometimes think we have a right to rewrite God's order. No, God is still in control, and even if you are a preacher, pastor, or prophet, you still have to go with His flow or be out of order. Until you get in God's order, your faith will never be perfected, and your miracle will never come.

James wrote to the churches:

> *What doth it profit, my brethren, though a man say he hath faith, and have not works? can faith save him? If a brother or sister be naked, and destitute of daily food, and one of you say unto them, Depart in peace, be ye warmed and filled; notwithstanding ye give them not those things which are needful to the body; what doth it profit? Even so faith, if it hath not works, is dead, being alone.*
>
> *Yea, a man may say, Thou hast faith, and I have works: shew me thy faith without thy works, and I will shew thee my faith by my works.*
>
> *Thou believest that there is one God; thou doest well: the devils also believe, and tremble. But wilt thou know, O vain man, that faith without works is dead? Was not Abraham our father justified by works, when he had offered Isaac his son upon the altar? Seest thou how faith wrought with his works, and by works was faith made perfect?*
>
> James 2:14-22

In other words, *"Go again seven times."* Going is a work, and that humble servant had to put his works with his faith. He did have faith on trip number four and five, but when he finally reached the seventh level, the bell was rung. He had pressed through every obstacle and won the victory. And you need to keep believing and keep pressing forward until the bell is rung for you, too.

James asked, *"Seest thou how faith wrought with his works, and by works was faith made perfect?"* It's an important question still today.

What was the conclusion?

> *And the scripture was fulfilled which saith, Abraham believed God, and it was imputed unto him for righteousness: and he was called the Friend of God. Ye see then how that by works a man is justified, and not by faith only.* James 2:23-24

By going and looking seven times the man was justified, not by faith alone. We can look ever so holy, but if we fail to go the second time and the third or however many times it takes, our faith is in vain. We can declare, "I believe the Lord," and we can make as many other confessions as we like, but if we fail to go again, we will not get our breakthrough. Confession is good, and that's a part of faith, but if the confessions are no accompanied by actions, nothing meaningful and lasting will come of them.

God has an order. Put your works with your faith and continue doing it until you have reached the seventh level. This is your responsibility. This is your duty. So don't try to rewrite the prescribed order of things.

James added:

> *Likewise also was not Rahab the harlot justified by works, when she had received the messengers, and had sent them out another way? For as the body without the spirit is dead, so faith without works is dead also.* James 2:25-26

If your spirit leaves you, you're dead, and *"faith without works is dead also."* Elijah and his servant have been long remembered because they included works with their faith. It was the same with our father Abraham. We remember him as a great man of faith, not only for what he believed, but for what he did because he believed. It's time for us to bring our faith to the seventh level, that level of perfection, of realization, of actualization. Press on to *The Seventh Level.*

## CHAPTER 5

# Bartimaeus Pressed to the Seventh Level

*And they came to Jericho: and as he went out of Jericho with his disciples and a great number of people, blind Bartimaeus, the son of Timaeus, sat by the highway side begging. And when he heard that it was Jesus of Nazareth, he began to cry out, and say, Jesus, thou son of David, have mercy on me.*

Mark 10:46-47

Not everyone was happy about the commotion this blind man was making, but Jesus was impressed, and that's what counts:

*And many charged him that he should hold his peace: but he cried the more a great deal, Thou son of David, have mercy on me. And Jesus stood still, and commanded him to be called.*

Mark 10:48-49

What this man did stopped Jesus in His tracks. The man may have been blind, but he understood God's order. This enabled him to ignore what others were saying and to concentrate on the Man who was passing by. He wasn't about to stop calling out after that first time. He refused to be quieted on the third time, and he only raised his voice another notch on the fifth time.

What was going on here? This little man was dealing with Nothing, but he somehow sensed that God was in his Nothing. Jesus was right there in the middle of the Nothing, and the blind man must not let this opportunity pass him by.

Blindness is a terrible thing, but it was blindness that brought this man to the seventh level. In his desperation, *"He cried out the more." This* impressed Jesus and stopped Him in His tracks. Then those around the blind man brought him some wonderful news:

> *Be of good comfort, rise; he calleth thee.*
>
> Mark 10:49

Those words represented the ringing of the bell. This blind man had won, even over the resistance of those around him, and he knew it. He instantly cast off his beggar's garments, for his faith had gone to the seventh level:

*And he, casting away his garment, rose, and came to Jesus.* Mark 10:50

Jesus asked the man what he wanted Him to do, and the man answered that he wanted to see. Jesus' answer was powerful:

*And Jesus said unto him, Go thy way; thy faith hath made thee whole. And immediately he received his sight, and followed Jesus in the way.* Mark 10:52

*"Thy faith hath made thee whole."* It was because the man had insisted on pressing into a higher level ... until he had reached the level of maturity and results.

When the Scriptures say, *"He cried out the more,"* most of us understand this to mean that he cried out one more time. But this word *more,* as used here, does not mean just one more time. It means "much." This man cried out and kept crying out until his answer came.

*"He cried out the more,"* is a very powerful phrase. How many times did he cry out? We don't know because the exact number is not given and is not important. The important thing is that he kept crying out until the bell rang.

I was shocked to discover, when I first studied this passage, that this term meant many, many, many more times. This *more* means "plenteous." Maybe it was seven times. The important thing is that he did not stop crying out until his answer came.

This phrase *all the more* simply means "to a greater degree." This man was determined. We get tired and give up, but he would not give up. People heard him crying out, and he didn't care who heard him crying out. And when they tried to stop him, he just cried out more.

You may have cried out five times or six, but don't give up. Press on to the next level. When your faith has reached the seventh level, guess what? Jesus will stand still for you, too, and you will have His full attention. But this type of victory demands pressing through the nothingness of your situation and perfecting your faith.

When Jesus said, *"Bring him here,"* many of those around him must have been surprised. Jesus had important places to go, important people to see, and important things to do. He stopped everything to signify to the crowd that this humble man had rung the bell.

Have you ever felt it when you rang the bell? I have. I knew it in that moment, and it's a wonderful feeling. But I'm sure you have also experienced the times of knowing that you just haven't broken through yet. Those are the moments when we must be careful not to give up or turn back. Pressing forward is our only option. What we do with Nothing will determined all of our tomorrows.

So what do you do with your Nothing? You must learn to look at your Nothing as if it already were Something. God is about to walk out of that Nothing and make it Something, but He is waiting on your faith to mature.

Why did this blind man receive his sight and other blind people remained in their blindness? Because he cried out the more. He cried out a great deal. He cried out more and more. He cried out as much as it took. He cried out until the answer came.

Do you know that God's order can be right there in the middle of your blindness, your darkness? Just look for it. It's there in the midst of every trial you face. If you can't yet cast off your darkness, at least embrace God's order in the midst of it. If you will dare to embrace God's order in your darkness, that darkness will sudden become light.

This man cried out the more, cried out a great deal, cried out until the bell was rung. Then, suddenly, he who could not see saw. He had not despised God's order, and now he reaped the fruits of his perfected faith.

But somehow he knew it before the first images hit his brain. He knew it when he first heard Jesus' words, *"Bring him to me."* He knew the bell had rung, and so he threw off that old garment. It was a new day.

Jesus knew it too, and so He said, "What would you like for Me to do for you?" The man could have asked for anything because his faith had reached that level of maturity.

I see two comparisons here: When Elijah and the servant saw the cloud the size of a man's hand, they knew their answer had come. The Lord had seen their perfected faith and was in the process of honoring it. What they saw was still small, but it didn't matter anymore. They knew how to see Something in their Nothing and more in their little. And the blessings of God can be brought to another level in your life too.

When Jesus saw that the blind man had perfected his faith, why would He ask him what he wanted? Didn't He know already? Oh, He did. Of course He did. But He wants us to determine our own futures and to declare them by faith.

When the man answered in this way, *"That I might see,"* immediately his blessing was brought to a new level. *"He received his sight."* Praise God! He will do it for you, too.

When there is Nothing, it simply means that God is up to Something, and we must move our faith to another level. The blind man brought his faith to the level of maturity and was rewarded.

I believe there comes a time when our faith is instantly perfected, but it requires that we take each of the steps of God's order. He graces us to go and look seven times, but we must be willing to do it. Then our answer comes.

May God grace you today. May His strength undergird you to press on to the seventh level. May you have supernatural endurance so that you can make it, whatever it may take to get there. May you march around your Jerichos until the walls fall flat.

May the graciousness, the kindness, the presence, the love, grace and mercy of God enable you to stand. May God Himself be your crutch, to walk with you, and to reveal to you the next round to fight, the next hill to climb, to bring your faith to that seventh level, that level of perfection.

May God be gracious to you, and may the brightness of His countenance be lifted up over you. Be encouraged today. Be lifted up. May the Lord be your Glory and the Lifter of your head.

Be not weary in your well-doing. Don't become weary after your fourth round. Don't be weary on your fifth trip of going and looking. Be not weary period. Don't give up. Don't lose heart. Be not weary in well-doing. In due season, you will reap if you don't faint first.

When will your *due season* arrive? When you have reached the seventh level. In your due season, you will be healed, delivered, and set free. Answers will come to you. You will reap — if you don't give up on the fifth level. God has said: *"He that endureth to the end shall be saved"* (Matthew 10:22). The same could be said for being healed, delivered, and brought through every other trial.

When the Scriptures say, *"Let us not be weary in well doing"* (Galatians 6:9), this *"well doing"* refers to your second, third, fourth, fifth, and sixth times of going and looking. And *going and looking* refers to your continual praise, praising God in spite of the trial, worshipping Him anyway, even when it is very hard to do. Do it anyway.

It's hard to worship God when great opposition arises against *you,* but that's when you must bring your confession and your faith to the next level. That's when you must look for God's order in the midst of your trial, and you must respectfully follow it.

Griping all the way doesn't count. We must be faithful until we're finally at that seventh level. Then the victory will come:

> *In due season we shall reap, if we faint not.*
>
> Galatians 6:9

Believe God's promise and press on to *The Seventh Level.*

## Chapter 6

# Our Creator Set the Example

*Thus the heavens and the earth were finished, and all the host of them. And on the seventh day God ended his work which he had made; and he rested on the seventh day from all his work which he had made. And God blessed the seventh day, and sanctified it: because that in it he had rested from all his work which God created and made.*

Genesis 2:1-3

Our journey to the seventh level began with the biblical truth: *"Now faith is the substance of things hoped for, the evidence of things not seen"* (Hebrews 11:1), and we asked the question: What do you do when there is nothing, no substance, no evidence? We discovered that God gives us a strategy to go about dealing with the area and atmosphere called Nothing, just plain old Nothing. And do you know what's worse than Nothing? Nothing! There is nothing worse than Nothing! Just plain old Nothing.

So what do you do when there is Nothing? As we discovered, God's Word says, *"Without faith it is impossible to please him"* (Hebrews 11:6), so we need to learn to move in faith, and the goal is to keep bringing our faith to the next level until it is eventually perfected and we receive what it is that we need from God.

As we have noted, inside of that atmosphere of Nothing really is Something, and it's because God created that Nothing. He created that space that we often consider to be Nothing. But when you get into the Spirit realm and the faith realm, all of a sudden you begin to see Something because God created that Nothing, and out of the Nothing comes Something. It is because God steps out of that Nothing in all of His manifested glory, and that's when things begin to happen.

This very day some of you who are reading this are dealing with a lot of Nothing, the seeming impossibilities of your daily existence. Be encouraged. The Bible says that Jesus is both the Author (the Originator) and the Finisher (the Perfecter) of our faith. God has a deep desire to perfect your faith, and in order to do that, He must create the Nothings you will deal with and overcome.

You must experience these Nothings. You must see them and then reach out to touch them, and when you do, you will feel nothing. This is important. You must experience Nothing so that you can be an overcomer in Christ.

## Our Creator Set the Example

Jesus, through His Word, creates and begins faith, and Jesus, through His Word, His ways, and His plans, perfects our faith. He tells us that we must lay hold of works and put them with our faith. The two must be mixed. One without the other is useless. We must put the two together like the elements of a mortar, and when we do that, Something will come out of the Nothing God created for our individual lives.

We can never point a finger at God and get mad at Him because there is Nothing. What do *you* do when there is Nothing? You'd better learn to do something and that something must be from God. He is waiting to take you to the seventh level.

From the very beginning God has worked with the number seven, beginning in the Old Testament and continuing right on through the New. As we have discovered, that number signifies completion.

Creation was a work of God's faith. He put works with His Spirit and with His words, and the result was that the worlds and all that is in them came into being. Faith originated with God, and He is a God of faith.

Our God is also a God of works. He does what He determines in faith, putting His words into meaningful actions. As an example, God said, *"Let there be light"* (Genesis 1:3), and it happened, and in this same way, He spoke all the rest of creation into existence. Then His Word declares: *"And on the seventh day God ended his work which he had made; and he rested on the seventh day from all his work which he had made."* He had worked for six days, and only when He reached the seventh day was it time to rest. You and I, in the same way, must bring our faith to the seventh level in order for it to be perfected. You can't stop halfway. You must bring your Christian experience — your faith and your works together— to the point of perfection, maturity, or realization.

God, not I, chose the number seven to signify completion, and since He chose it, I have to deal with it. He rested on the seventh day, and we can too.

But there is more: *"Then God blessed the seventh day."* He actually had His own personal ceremony. Isn't that amazing!

I know where that wonderful word *WOW* came from. When God looked out over all that He had created, He said it: "WOW!" Nothing else could explain such a wonderful creation. Just "WOW!"

Then God had to decide what to do next, and the Bible says that He decided to bless that seventh day. This word *blessed* means that He praised it. It means that He saluted every star in the sky.

Some time ago now I saw on the news that scientists, using a very powerful telescope, have discovered another large galaxy with millions of stars in it. They said that it was several billions of light years old, and I can believe that because God is a lot older than that. As they build bigger and more powerful telescopes, they will continue to find more and more of this marvelous creation. It goes on and on. Do you think God would ever allow man to discover the limits of His creation? Never. Do you ever wonder how far it all goes? Let's just say that it is far beyond our ability to comprehend.

God blessed, or saluted, His creation. In other words, He congratulated it. He was not and is not a God of pride, so He could handle that. He said, "I congratulate, I salute, My creation." He did this on the seventh day, and He blessed that day and made it special.

Why was the seventh day so special? For six days God had spoken things into existence one after the other. On Day 1, He said, *"Let there be,"* and there was. On Day 2, He spoke, and there was, and this continued day after day. In this way, our wonderful God set an example for us by pressing on to the seventh day and then declaring that day special.

When God made it to the seventh day, there was rest, and there was celebration. He saluted His creation, and He blessed the day that had completed it. And, from that day forward, the seventh day was special. What does this mean to us today on a practical level? It means that you and I must make it to the seventh level. We must persevere until our faith is perfected, matured, or completed.

In God's act of adoration that day was the sense of knowing that what He was seeing was definitely real. It existed, and His faith had brought it about. So He blessed that day.

Then He went further: He *sanctified* that day and pronounced it holy. This was all done in God's own personal ceremonial dedication, and it happened on the seventh day.

It was all symbolic of what happens when you bring your faith (accompanied by the appropriate works) to the seventh level. That is when you can rest, and the works of your hands done in response to your faith can then be blessed.

On the third and the fourth level, there may be faith, and there must be works, but it will not yet be completed. Your faith exists, and it is growing, but it cannot yet rest in accomplishment. You haven't yet made it to the day when your faith and the accompanying works can be blessed and become holy.

You might say, "But I'm working for the Lord." That may be true, but those works are not necessarily in the atmosphere of holiness.

You might say, "I have faith," but is it holy faith? You need to have holy faith. You need sanctified faith. On levels one and two, it's definitely not yet sanctified. You have a long way to go. You haven't made it yet.

God was our example. He held the seventh day to be special, holy, sanctified.

## Our Creator Set the Example

Let's take another look at that text:

> *And God blessed the seventh day, and sanctified it; because that in it he had rested from all his work which God created and made.* Genesis 2:3

This word *created* has to do with the beginning, but the word *made* has to do with all the things God had accomplished. His work was finalized.

When He created, it took Him six days, but on that seventh day, He no longer needed to create. When He stepped into that seventh day, it was time to rest. He had made it all.

If God had been like us, He could have been hung up until now on that sixth day wondering if He had done it right. Should He go back to the fifth day and do it over? But, no, God stepped over into the seventh day, and He knew that it was finished. So now He blessed it, and He sanctified it, because it was an accomplished work. All things had been finalized.

Oh, how God wants the Church to come into that seventh level of our faith and our accompanying works, where we can say, "It is blessed! It is sanctified! It is finished! It is completed!" That's when you can offer your hallelujahs, and they will be holy.

God rested on the seventh day, and when you and I are able to bring our works and faith to the seventh level, there will be a rest that comes to us as well. We will ring the bell, knowing that our faith is perfected. It has been sanctified, and we can come into our promised rest.

So don't stop now, beloved. Let's press on to *The Seventh Level.*

CHAPTER 7

# The Seventh Level in the Ancient Law

*And they brought seven bullocks, and seven rams, and seven lambs, and seven he goats, for a sin offering for the kingdom, and for the sanctuary, for Judah. And he commanded the priests the sons of Aaron to offer them on the altar of the* LORD.

2 Chronicles 29:21

God used the number seven in temple worship. He chose that number seven to signify well done, and with it He put the people of Israel to the test. When they began choosing bullocks, rams, lambs, and goats for an offering to Him, they could not be satisfied with one, two, three, four, five, or six. They could not stop sacrificing unto Him until He was happy with their sacrifice, and His required number was seven. So it had to be seven. Nothing less would do.

But sacrificing is not always easy, and we can imagine that when some had chosen out the best five or six of their beloved animals and set them apart for sacrifice, they must have been tempted to stop with that good number. Six was good enough, after all, or maybe even five. That seventh one they had eyed was the pick of the litter, and they would need to feed their families in the months ahead and have good stock for breeding new generations. Maybe they should just keep it.

The more they thought about it, the more that seventh one somehow seemed to be the best formed and best looking of the lot. They had some sickly-looking animals. Some had bad eyes or torn ears. But that seventh one was absolutely perfect. Surely God would not expect them to sacrifice the most perfect one. But that was exactly what God was requiring. He didn't want the second best, only the perfect.

What does this mean to us today? You can't stop worshipping God. You can't give Him less than your best. You can't stop when it comes to making a sacrifice to Him. When things get tough and it looks like there is nothing, that's when you need to give God your best worship. Give Him that seventh sacrifice. Bring your faith and your works, bring your sacrifice, bring your music, bring your voice, bring your hands, and bring your dance to the seventh level.

Even in the temple worship, God used the number seven, and it is still meaningful to us today.

In the book of Revelation it talks about the *"seven churches"* (Revelation 1:4, 11 and 20), the *"seven Spirits"* (Revelation 1:4, 3:1, 4:5 and 5:6), the *"seven golden candlesticks"* (Revelation 1:12, 20 and 2:1), *"seven stars"* (Revelation 1:16, 20, 2:1 and 3:1), *"seven lamps"* (Revelation 4:5), *"seven seals"* (Revelation 5:1 and 5), *"seven horns"* and *"seven eyes"* (Revelation 5:6), *"seven angels"* (Revelation 8:2, 6, 15:1, 6-8, 16:1, 17:1 and 21:9), *"seven trumpets"* (Revelation 8:2 and 6), *"seven thunders"* (Revelation 10:3-4), *"seven plagues"* (Revelation 15:6 and 8), *"seven vials"* (Revelation 17:1 and 21:9), *"seven heads"* (Revelation 12:3, 13:1, 17:3, 7 and 9), and *"seven mountains"* (Revelation 17:9). God seems to be hung up on seven. Why is that? It's because He wants to see your faith perfected.

God works through the number seven. He did it in Bible days, and He continues to do it today in us. If we fail to relate this message to our own personal lives, then what good is it? Let God's order touch you where you live today.

David was inspired to sing:

> *The words of the* LORD *are pure words: as silver tried in a furnace of earth, purified seven times.*
>
> Psalm 12:6

Silver was purified seven times. Why did it take seven times for it to be purified? Because seven is the number indicating the completion of any process. Look at it for yourself throughout the Bible.

This verse refers to the sevenfold trying and testing of God's Word itself. When His Word is being tried, it happens through you and through me, and that is by God's design. He welcomes His Word being tested through us. He welcomes His Word being tested through you. Why? Because He wants you to bring your faith to the seventh level, and in order for that to happen, His Word must get involved, that Word that you have purposefully and willfully hidden inside of your heart.

This is not a word that you try to find somewhere. It is not a word that you run to some prophet to get. This is the Word that you have hidden in your heart. That Word must be tried and retried. Did you think you would experience a single trial and overcome by the Word hidden in you and that would be it? Oh, no!

Have you noticed that things are getting worse and worse in the world's system? Have you noticed that things are closing in on the Church? Well, expect more trials ahead. God's Word must be tested and tried in you, even until seven times.

There is a process with the Word, a process with our faith, and that process requires regular testing. So get ready for more of it, and it doesn't get any easier.

Jesus is the Finisher of our faith, and He uses His Word to do the needed work. He uses His faith in us and through us to bring our spirits to the place of maturity. So in order to go to the seventh level, you must bring your spirit along with you.

On this journey, your spirit must be a right and clean one, and you must make this journey with a right and clean attitude. If you are to bring your faith and your works to the level of perfection, because your spirit is all tied up with your faith, that spirit must match up with your faith and your works. None of them can be bad. One of them might be good, but if another is ugly or "messed up," then your faith and works cannot be blessed, they cannot be sanctified, and you will have no rest. Bring yourself along in the right way, praising God out of a heart of love and worship, and in due time, you will be amply rewarded.

*"The words of the Lord are pure as silver tried in a furnace of earth, purified seven times."* God desires that our faith be perfected. Therefore we must bring our faith to that seventh level. This means that we must allow it to be passed through the fire seven times, until the purifying process is complete.

Why is fire used? Fire burns. Fire purges. Fire purifies. Fire brings out feelings. I dare you to bring your faith to the next level, to press on until you have reached the level of perfection, to pass your faith through the fires and keep on doing it until you have reached that seventh level of purity. I guarantee you that you will experience a day of blessing, a day of saluting, celebration, sanctification, and rest. In that moment, you will be a testimony. You will be a sign and a wonder to the world around you.

Stand firm until that day. Press on to *The Seventh Level.*

## Chapter 8

# A Seventh-Level Trial

*Then Nebuchadnezzar in his rage and fury commanded to bring Shadrach, Meshach, and Abednego. Then they brought these men before the king.*

Daniel 3:13

This took place in the time of the prophet Daniel. It is worthwhile for us to review the entire passage to gain a better perspective on what was happening that enraged this king and what he did about it that affected Daniel's three young friends:

*Nebuchadnezzar the king made an image of gold, whose height was threescore cubits, and the breadth thereof six cubits: he set it up in the plain of Dura, in the province of Babylon. Then Nebuchadnezzar the king sent to gather together the princes, the governors, and the captains, the judges, the treasurers, the counsellors, the sheriffs, and all the rulers of the provinces, to come to the dedication of the image which Nebuchadnezzar the king had set up. Then the princes, the governors, and captains, the judges, the treasurers, the counsellors, the sheriffs, and all the rulers of the provinces, were gathered together unto the dedication of the image that Nebuchadnezzar the king had set up; and they stood before the image that Nebuchadnezzar had set up.*

*Then an herald cried aloud, To you it is commanded, O people, nations, and languages, that at what time ye hear the sound of the cornet, flute, harp, sackbut, psaltery, dulcimer, and all kinds of musick, ye fall down and worship the golden image that Nebuchadnezzar the king hath set up: and whoso falleth not down and worshippeth shall the same hour be cast into the midst of a burning fiery furnace.*

*Therefore at that time, when all the people heard the sound of the cornet, flute, harp, sackbut, psaltery, and all kinds of musick, all the people, the nations, and the languages, fell down and worshipped the golden image that Nebuchadnezzar the king had set up.*

*Wherefore at that time certain Chaldeans came near, and accused the Jews. They spake and said to the king Nebuchadnezzar, O king, live for ever. Thou, O king, hast made a decree, that every man that shall hear the sound of the cornet, flute, harp, sackbut, psaltery, and dulcimer, and all kinds of musick, shall fall down and worship the golden image: and whoso falleth not down and worshippeth, that he should be cast into the midst of a burning fiery furnace. There are certain Jews whom thou hast set over the affairs of the province of Babylon, Shadrach, Meshach, and Abednego; these men, O king, have not regarded thee: they serve not thy gods, nor worship the golden image which thou hast set up. Then Nebuchadnezzar in his rage and fury commanded to bring Shadrach, Meshach, and Abednego. Then they brought these men before the king.* Daniel 3:1-13

So that was what had enraged the king, and now let's see what he, in his rage, chose to do about it:

*Nebuchadnezzar spake and said unto them, Is it true, O Shadrach, Meshach, and Abednego, do not ye serve my gods, nor worship the golden image which I have set up? Now if ye be ready that at what time ye hear the sound of the cornet, flute, harp, sackbut, psaltery, and dulcimer, and all kinds of musick, ye fall down and worship the image which I have made; well: but if ye worship not, ye shall be cast the same hour into the midst of a burning fiery furnace; and who is that God that shall deliver you out of my hands?*
*Shadrach, Meshach, and Abednego, answered and said to the king, O Nebuchadnezzar, we are not careful to answer thee in this matter. If it be so, our God*

> *whom we serve is able to deliver us from the burning fiery furnace, and he will deliver us out of thine hand, O king. But if not, be it known unto thee, O king, that we will not serve thy gods, nor worship the golden image which thou hast set up.*
>
> Daniel 3:14-18

Everyone thought that Nebuchadnezzar was as mad as could be, but now he got even angrier:

> *Then was Nebuchadnezzar full of fury, and the form of his visage was changed against Shadrach, Meshach, and Abednego: therefore he spake, and commanded that they should heat the furnace one seven times more than it was wont to be heated.*
>
> Daniel 3:19

There are some things Christians must never do — trial or no trial, threat of no threat — and one of them it to bow before other gods. These three men knew better, and so they were not about to go there. It didn't matter to them who was commanding it or what the threat was. They were not about to obey, and before serious trials come your way, you, too, need to make a firm decision that nothing will separate you from your God. *"We will not,"* these men said, and you must make that same declaration.

These three men were determined not to rob God of His glory, even if it cost them their lives. They had seen this trial coming and knew what it meant, and still they had made up their minds to do the right thing. They knew the price, and yet they refused to worship anyone or anything that was not the true and living God.

In light of the determination of these three Hebrew boys, it mystifies me when I see some of God's modern-day people getting sloppy with their worship of Him. May God help us in this critical hour not to bow the knee to this world's demands. They said, *"We will not serve thy gods, nor worship the golden image."* What is your determination? Have you made some declarations about your personal life and about the family members you are responsible for?

Many Christians desperately need to set their houses in order. They need to declare, "I will not allow my children to run wild, disrespect me, and do their own thing and me just sit by in fear and helplessness." God is requiring such a commitment on our part.

Mommas and daddys, you'd better rise up and set your house in order. Start with yourself, and then set the rest straight before it's too late and the test has overtaken you and your loved ones.

Some of you parents have been so slouchy and slothful that it's no wonder your children are misbehaving. Some of you are failing to take charge of your house and to put the proper discipline in place. You need to declare, even as Joshua, *"As for me and my house, we will serve the LORD,"* (Joshua 24:15).

The three Hebrew boys of Daniel's time made such a decree, and it helped them. It prepared them for the next stage.

Nebuchadnezzar, of course, was not happy about their commitment. He acted just like the devil who was in him: *"Then was Nebuchadnezzar full of fury, and the form of his visage was changed against Shadrach, Meshach, and Abednego."* His face was contorted, and he must have been an ugly man about that time. Anger and meanness and evil make people so much uglier than they really are. Now, in his anger, Nebuchadnezzar issued the fateful command: *"Therefore he spake, and commanded that they should heat the furnace one seven times more than it was wont to be heated."*

*"Seven times more"* ... Why would God have allowed this? Because of the high call to ministry that was upon the lives of these three boys. It was just that powerful. By this act, God was saying, "Boys, you have come a long way, you have done well, and you have pleased Me, but because of what I see ahead for you, what I have called you to become, I have to put this seventh issue before you. I must bring you through this higher trial. You must face this test in order to bring your faith to the seventh level."

So God allowed this thing to happen. He permitted the king to try them in this way. Therefore we must conclude that this was all part of God's order of things. Get used to it. God has destined us to be tested, but He has also destined us to overcome every test.

When the king said, *"till seven times,"* this word *times* means "order." This was the order of God, or the times of God. The king thought he was devising this whole plan in his anger, but God devised it to gain glory for Himself and enlarge His Kingdom.

The phrase *seven times* used here was in reference to "beyond that which was fit, beyond that which was necessary." And who decides what is necessary? This was an exceptional test, but the fact that God allowed it signifies that He, at least, thought it was necessary. King Nebuchadnezzar could not have thrown God's children into a burning furnace if God had not permitted him to do it. So God allowed the king to test His boys in this way.

Isn't it unusual that a pagan king, in a moment of rage, would think of the number seven? God did that. If not, how did that particular phrase get into the king's mind and into his vocabulary? It is amazing what God allows to perfect His people.

It took seven times, not just five or six, to get the heat of the furnace to its greatest intensity. That was mighty hot, but it was necessary. It was a must, a requirement, a "have to." God had a purpose for it.

As far as we can tell from history, this king had never before ordered his ovens to be heated to their seventh level. But then he had never before dealt with God's chosen ones, His anointed Jews. Specifically, he had never dealt with Shadrach, Meshach, and Abednego before.

When Nebuchadnezzar commanded the furnace to be heated seven times hotter that day, he surely could not have realized its total significance, but God knew what He was doing. He wanted this oven to be at its highest possible intensity because He had some faith to purge and make perfect.

When the king decreed: *"Heat the furnace one seven times more than it was wont to be heated,"* this word *one* is an interesting word, and the reason he said, *"Heat the furnace one seven times"* is powerful. When they pushed up the heat one time, they brought it to the next level, much as we would turn up a thermostat in our homes. When you kick that thermostat up to the next level, the furnace responds, and the house immediately starts getting warmer. You can push that thermostat up as many degrees as you want, and the temperature will continue to rise ... until it reaches the desired level.

When the king said, *"one seven times,"* he meant: "Bring it up to every level at once. Bring it to level five, level six, and level seven ... until they all become one. Do it all at the same time." This was a command to hurry up the usual heating process and bring the furnace to its greatest capacity all at once. The king's servants were to heat that furnace until it could not get any hotter, and this is where God wants to bring our faith and our works today.

So, level by level by level, the thermostat was going up, up, and up, and then, all of a sudden, it had reached its maximum level. It was at *"one seven times,"* and that was when something wonderful happened.

At this point, the king called for some of his strongest men:

> *And he commanded the most mighty men that were in his army to bind Shadrach, Meshach, and Abednego, and to cast them into the burning fiery furnace.* Daniel 3:20

Shadrach, Meshach and Abednego heard what the king said. They had heard him when he said to heat the oven seven times. They had watched as the servants quickly put on more and more fuel, and the temperature continued to rise. At any point in the process, they could have recanted their bold declaration and begged the king for mercy, but they did not. As the heat rose, their faith continued to rise with it. As the test rose from level to level, their faith rose to match it.

Now they heard the king tell strong men to bind them, and they watched as those men approached. This may have been another opportunity to recant their words and turn back, but again they did not. Their faith was rising to the occasion.

As the level of heat rose, they felt it and had a decision to make. Their faith had continued to rise with the heat of every level of the trial.

At one point, Shadrach may have said, "Hey, Abednego, the heat is on the fifth level. Do you think we should recant?"

"No," would have come the answer, "we have come this far by faith, and we can't turn back now."

Then Meshach said, "Shadrach, it's at the sixth level. Can we stand it?"

"God is with us regardless," came the answer.

Their faith was experiencing every level, but this trial was developing fast. Did you ever get into a trial that was moving fast? The heat is rushing at you, and you're not sure what you should do. Some trials develop very slowly, but others come rushing at us. Personally I don't like to be rushed, but sometimes we don't have a choice. We are not the one controlling the trial; God is.

This time, even as the heat was rushing at them, the king was urging his men to hurry up the process even more, get the furnace hot faster, push it to its limit, let it happen all at once. And all of this was what those boys were experiencing. Their faith had to rise with each degree rise in temperature. If they had stood it thus far, they could stand the rest, and so they persevered. They were made to stand there at the ready as the heat was pushed higher and higher in response to the king's furor, and they endured, gaining strength from level to level, sure now that they could survive this ordeal.

As the tests came at them faster, their faith responded, and with this I must issue a warning to the Church: Trials will come upon us in the near future in such rapid succession that we will feel overwhelmed if we are not ready for them. Get ready. Don't let your faith become rusty. Cast off that arthritic faith, for your faith must move from level to level in accordance with the trials that come your way. Get ready for your special testings. Let your faith loose, and let it be ready to move fast, to come to that seventh level, that your faith may be perfected and completed.

The climax of the situation soon occurred:

> *Then these men were bound in their coats, their hosen, and their hats, and their other garments, and were cast into the midst of the burning fiery furnace. Therefore because the king's commandment was urgent, and the furnace exceeding hot, the flames of the fire slew those men that took up Shadrach, Meshach, and Abednego. And these*

> *three men, Shadrach, Meshach, and Abednego, fell down bound into the midst of the burning fiery furnace.*
> *Then Nebuchadnezzar the king was astonished, and rose up in haste, and spake, and said unto his counsellors, Did not we cast three men bound into the midst of the fire?*
> *They answered and said unto the king, True, O king.*
> *He answered and said, Lo, I see four men loose, walking in the midst of the fire, and they have no hurt; and the form of the fourth is like the Son of God.*
> *Then Nebuchadnezzar came near to the mouth of the burning fiery furnace ... .* Daniel 3:21-24

This was another notable miracle. Did you notice that when the strong men threw the Hebrew boys into the fire those same men were slain by the intensity of the heat? The king, on the other hand, was preserved, even though he *"came near to the mouth of the burning fiery furnace."* God was gracious to that mean old devil and gave him the opportunity to turn his life around. What a miracle that was!

When the king approached the flames, he was amazed to see the men he had determined to burn up loose and walking around in the fire. Now his tone changed dramatically, and he called them forth from the fire:

> *Then Nebuchadnezzar ... spake, and said, Shadrach, Meshach, and Abednego, ye servants of the most high God, come forth, and come hither.* Daniel 3:26

Amazingly, they did just that. And now they were suddenly a powerful witness to those around them, including the powerful Nebuchadnezzar:

> *And the princes, governors, and captains, and the king's counsellors, being gathered together, saw these men, upon whose bodies the fire had no power, nor was an hair of their head singed, neither were their coats changed, nor the smell of fire had passed on them.*
>
> *Then Nebuchadnezzar spake, and said, Blessed be the God of Shadrach, Meshach, and Abednego, who hath sent his angel, and delivered his servants that trusted in him, and have changed the king's word, and yielded their bodies, that they might not serve nor worship any god, except their own God.*
>
> Daniel 3:27-28

Oh, wow! Tests have a purpose. They not only purify you; they also make you an effective witness for your faith.

To make a long story short, this heathen king, Nebuchadnezzar, now turned to God, and he then made a decree to be sent throughout the whole land that everybody (including himself) would serve the God of Shadrach, Meshach, and Abednego. Wow! Oh, wow! Can you sense why such revival and such a move of God came to this heathen king and his men? It was because three boys allowed their faith to go to the highest, hottest level.

The hottest level is never the first, and it's not the fourth or the fifth. It is the seventh level, the level of perfecting or maturing. There will be times when your tests will hit you so hard and so fast that your head will be spinning, but if you remain faithful to God, before you know it, that trial will be over, and God will get the glory. Restoration and healing can come to your whole family if you'll just stand firm in your faith and refuse to back down. Instead of a reproach to the Gospel, you will become a mighty voice for the Lord and His Kingdom.

These boys did not back down, and they did not doubt God. As they stood in each moment of trial, their faith was being perfected. Suddenly they were thrown into that seventh level of heat, that seventh level of trial, and that seventh level of testing, but they came out of it whole and blessed. They had been ready to die if that became necessary, but God had something else in mind. He wanted to be glorified in their trial and to win many others to Himself.

God wants to perfect your faith, and the only way He can do it is for you to face the purifying fires of life.

Would you let Him do His work in you today? Take hold of your works, and say, "Works, we are going to the next level. It may be hot, and the pressures may come upon us fast, but God will grace us, because we really do want our faith to be perfected."

Pray, "Lord, in this hour of Your move in the earth, when You are demonstrating Your power in miracles, signs, and wonders, grace us to experience where the glory is. It is only to be found in the seventh level. Only at that level can we be blessed and sanctified and enjoy Your rest."

God will be glorified when our faith is perfected, and then others can be healed and blessed as well. A heathen king was saved that day at the mouth of the furnace he had intended for harm because three Hebrew boys stood the test of faith. This, then, brought many others into the Kingdom.

May God grace each of us to stand and not turn back. Let us pray, "We trust You, Lord Jesus. May this word burn within every one of us. We can no longer be hearers only. We must be doers of Your Word, with faithfulness, commitment, and loyalty." Amen!

Now press on to *The Seventh Level*.

CHAPTER 9

# Taking Your Blessings to the Seventh Level

*Then spake Elisha unto the woman, whose son he had restored to life, saying, Arise, and go thou and thine household, and sojourn wheresoever thou canst sojourn; for the* LORD *hath called for a famine; and it shall also come upon the land seven years.*

2 Kings 8:1

Is this story about the seventh level too? Yes, it is. Let the Word of the Lord penetrate your heart today and lift you up to a higher level.

This is a very unusual story. A prophet of God was not prophesying blessing and favor, but, instead, warning a good and godly woman to take all she had and run, and he didn't even tell her where to go. *"Wheresoever thou canst sojourn"* did not see like much guidance, but that was all that was forthcoming.

So what did this woman do? Being the woman of faith that she was, she obeyed without question:

> *And the woman arose, and did after the saying of the man of God: and she went with her household, and sojourned in the land of the Philistines seven years.* 2 Kings 8:2

That doesn't sound very appealing, but God had something good in mind. He wanted to test this woman because He had some blessings in store for her. If we will abide in the will of God and be faithful in our obedience, our loyalty, and our commitment, life will be strewn with divine events like this one. There are events and experiences all along our way, and they can turn into divine events, demonstrating and proving the providence of an Almighty God.

There are certain specially planned-out and predetermined events that God allows and releases on you and for you. Nothing happens in our lives apart from His divine appointments or permissions.

Do you think for a moment that God is dumb, that He is somehow ignorant? Oh no, *"His way is* perfect:

> *As for God, his way is perfect.* 2 Samuel 22:31

> *... his work is perfect.* Deuteronomy 32:14

For those who are faithful and determined to be obedient to God, behind every event and incident there is divine providence waiting, there is divine guidance, and there is divine provision.

In this passage of scripture, the man of God speaks to a little woman, who had already experienced God's power in supernatural signs and wonders. But not everything went well in her life. The fourth chapter records the fact that her son had died, and she had a less than spiritual spouse. Some of you might relate to that. But God raised that boy up.

This woman experienced miracles just because she was obedient, faithful, and in tune with God. You have to get with the program. Get in there with God and learn His program, and you, too, will see signs and wonders.

"Does God have a program?" some might ask. He definitely does, and He wants to show Himself strong on your behalf. He's just waiting for you to get onboard.

Because God loves you, He permits you to be tempted and tested, but He has promised to keep you through every test and trial. Even as a new test now came to this woman, God was about to bless her even more.

The prophet of God told the woman to leave Israel. The country was in trouble. A famine was coming, so he told her to get out and go wherever she could find a place to live.

Most of us would not have liked to receive such a word. We would want much more detail, but no more detail was forthcoming. This was a serious test of the woman's faith. Her faith and her obedience were about to be introduced to the greatest trial of her life. *"Sojourn [or live] wherever you can,"* the man had said, and that was all she knew.

When words come to us without details, it forces to us to lean on God, to truly trust Him for wisdom, for guidance, and for provision for every step of the way. The prophet foretold a famine and said to her, in the lingo of today, "Get out while you can, and go wherever you can go."

And it got worse. He told her to stay gone for seven years. Wow! Seven long years in exile. That was a hard test.

Did this woman argue with the prophet? Did she protest such a vague word? She didn't, and that says a lot about her. Instead, she *"arose and did after the saying of the man of God."* No wonder she was blessed!

The woman now chose to live among the Philistines and settled in a place where she knew absolutely no one. The Philistines were strange people, but they knew how to raise crops, so at least she and her family would eat well.

Not everyone living in that place was a Philistine. There was a mixture of peoples, many of them illegal immigrants who had sneaked in, trying to survive the famine. Most of them had made the decision to go there on their own, but this woman was sent there by God with a divine purpose (that was yet to be revealed).

God had not given her express instructions, but she knew that He was with her and would prosper her wherever she went, and something made her believe that the land of the Philistines was the right place. So she set out, believing that God would meet her there.

This woman went out much like Abraham, *"not knowing whither [s]he went"* (Hebrews 11:8). She ended up in the land of the Philistines, and sure enough, God was there waiting for her. He said, "Hello," and she said, "Hello," and she and her household were there for the next seven years.

This was blind faith and obedience. She had heard two things that didn't sound good to her at all. She had heard the word *famine,* and she had heard *seven years*. Those facts would have troubled a lot of us. This was a serious trial of faith, but what choice did she have? God had ordained this trial for His glory.

As with all trials, this one came to an end, and there was a turnaround, a return:

*And it came to pass at the seven years' end, that the woman returned out of the land of the Philistines.*
2 Kings 8:3

But this turnaround was a long time coming, and in the meantime, life had to go on. I can just imagine how hard life among the Philistines must have been for the first six months. The woman and her family were strangers in a strange land, and no doubt everyone wanted to take advantage of them, few wanted to befriend them, and they had no one to turn to in times of need. That was rough.

When the first year was completed, it must have been a relief. They had survived a whole year of their ordeal. On the other hand, the woman knew that she still had six more years to go. Could she and her family withstand six more years of such trials?

Friend, there is a seventh level that we all need to reach with our faith. Many places in the Bible reveal that level, and we are constantly being challenged to go higher and to eventually bring our faith to maturity and effectiveness. When that seventh level is finally experienced, and the bell is rung, something supernatural happens. It happens first in your spirit, and then your surroundings are affected by it. And this is how your faith is perfected.

Again, Jesus is the Author and Finisher or Perfecter of our faith, but our faith cannot grow without challenge, and it takes bringing our faith to that seventh level to have it matured and perfected.

The Bible says in that third verse, *"And it came to pass at the seven years' end ... ."* I can imagine that the circumstances of a widow living in a strange land must have been declining year after year. Things were getting worse for her and her family. The third year was worse than the second, and the fifth year was worse than the fourth. But when that fifth year had finally ended, she had no choice but to persevere into the sixth year. Her goal was seven years, and she must make it to the final hour of the final day.

Surely she must have been tempted many times to go back, to try something else, to do something different, but the man of God had said that she should live abroad and that she should do so for seven years. So, by God's grace, she would stay seven years, not a day less.

There was a purpose in all of this. God had a plan. If she could be faithful for seven years, surely the supernatural and the providential were out there waiting for her.

When she reached that seventh year, the nights must have been interminable. Have you ever noticed that tests are much harder at night, when it's the darkest? You look out the window, and there is nothing to be seen, just the blackness of the night surrounding you. In those lonely hours, she must have been tempted to give up.

There can be no doubt that the seventh year was the hardest, and the days dragged by. Those midnight hours were intolerable. Could she overcome this? Could she survive it?

In the darkest hour, Satan is in his element. He comes to you and taunts you, "Why not give up. There is no way you can survive this." Or he suggests some more "reasonable" alternative. But if your faith is intact, your spirit looks out and pierces through that nothingness, that darkness, and sees the light of day. Then joy breaks through.

All of sudden, you're singing, "Joy, joy, joy!" It has hit you like a ton of bricks. *"Joy comes in the morning"*:

> *For his anger endureth but a moment; in his favour is life: weeping may endure for a night, but joy cometh in the morning.* Psalm 30:5

If your morning has not yet dawned, know that joy is on the way. If you can persevere a little longer, supernatural joy will be your portion.

You can know this even when you're in the midst of your nothings and your darkness. That's when you have to stick and stay and not play. Joy is coming. Count on it. Expect it. Wait for it. Be faithful until it breaks through your darkness.

When the seven years ended, because this woman was a person of faith and obedience, and because of her tenacity, her stickability, her saying, "I'm in this for the long haul," her victory came: *"And it came to pass at the seven years' end, that the woman returned out of the land of the Philistines."*

Jesus said:

> *He that endureth to the end shall be saved.*
> Matthew 10:22

Paul wrote:

> *I press toward the mark for the prize of the high calling of God in Christ Jesus.* Philippians 3:14

> *Fight the good fight of faith, lay hold on eternal life.* 1 Timothy 6:12

> *Having done all, ... stand.* Ephesians 6:13

Therefore we know that we can remain faithful until we have reached the seventh level. We can face the test until the final hour and gain a victory.

I believe that this little woman knew something that a lot of churches and modern-day saints haven't yet learned: God has reserved the best for us, and it is yet to come. That may seem like an overworked phrase, but it is more true today than ever before. The best is yet to come.

There was an interesting twist to this story. It's not just a story of repatriation. This woman was expecting much more, and because of her faith and obedience, she would have much more.

> *And she went forth to cry unto the king for her house and for her land.* 2 Kings 8:3

No sooner had the woman arrived home than she went straight to the palace to put forth a petition before the king. Evidently she noticed, when she got back to her house and land, that someone had taken it over in her absence and had been farming the land and living in the house. She wanted it all back. These squatters must have made some money that rightfully belonged to her, and she wanted that back too. Her faith was stronger than ever. She had endured seven years of hardship and survived, so she knew what God could do.

She was now kicked into overdrive and was ready to roll. She was fearless and decided to go for it. She went to the palace to demand the return of her house and land.

What a turnaround! What a great turnaround! Seven years of obedience had given this woman such a foundation of encouragement that her faith was soaring. Each year that she had survived and persevered took her higher until she had now entered into that seventh level, and she would not and could not be denied.

There was a new special layer covering her, an icing if you will, and she was ready to face the king and boldly plead her cause.

Only this woman's faith qualified her for complete restoration. We must remember that she was a woman living in a man's world. Even in our modern times, women often have to fight for their rights, but in those days, they had very few rights at all. Now, as this woman marched to the palace, God did a great miracle:

> *And the king talked with Gehazi the servant of the man of God, saying, Tell me, I pray thee, all the great things that Elisha hath done. And it came to pass, as he was telling the king how he had restored a dead body to life, that, behold, the woman, whose son he had restored to life, cried to the king for her house and for her land. And Gehazi said, My lord, O king, this is the woman, and this is her son, whom Elisha restored to life.*
>
> 2 Kings 8:4-5

Can you imagine it! At the very moment this woman was approaching the palace, the king was asking Gehazi, the prophet's servant, about the mighty deeds the prophet had done, and Gehazi was telling the king how God had restored her son to life. Then Gehazi saw her, and said to the king, *"This is the woman."* Wasn't that a coincidence?

Gehazi must have been amazed by the change that had come over this woman. With seven years of hardship and stubborn overcoming under her belt, she was a new woman. She had been a tough lady before, but now her toughness had multiplied many times over, and all because her faith had risen to a new level.

The woman's request put the king in a difficult legal position. There existed then, as now, what is called Squatter's Rights. If a person lived on a piece of land and farmed it, they could then lay legal claim to it. But no squatter was going to get away with cheating this woman out of her land.

Does this have something to do with us today? Yes, it does. The devil will take over your home, your marriage, your children, your finances, your physical body, and then he will boldly declare that he has claimed them all as his own. He will insist that you have forfeited all legal rights and so he is now in charge. Let's tell the Squatter to go back to the pit where he came from.

Jesus said:

> *The thief cometh not, but for to steal, and to kill, and to destroy: I am come that they might have life, and that they might have it more abundantly.*
>
> John 10:10

With the Kingdom of God, no squatter's rights are recognized. As God's children, we have our rights and our legal grounds for action. No enemy can lay claim to what is ours and get away with it. Let's boldly stand our ground.

Seven years of suffering and perseverance had now brought this little woman to the point of declaring: "I want my house and land, and I want it now."

*And when the king asked the woman, she told him.*
2 Kings 8:6

Would you have been intimidated by the presence of a king? Most of us would, but not this woman. She knew who she was and what she wanted, and she was going to get it — no matter what. And she did get it:

*So the king appointed unto her a certain officer, saying, Restore all that was hers, and all the fruits of the field since the day that she left the land, even until now.* 2 Kings 8:6

The king had no excuses that day. Without argument, he restored all to her. She got back not only her house and lands, but also the proceeds from the sale of her crops. "Make sure," I hear the king telling his officer, "that she gets paid everything she has coming to her." Praise God!

When the spirit of restoration begins to work, it is amazing to see what God will do. Do you know how to spell restoration? It is spelled with three little letters: A-L-L. God included all the fruit of the land and the field because this woman of faith had stepped into that seventh year.

When you have willfully left something, when you have purposely walked away, believe me the enemy will waste no time establishing rights over it. But God is showing us that we can come back and reclaim what is ours, if we have matured in our faith and risen to new levels.

I'm sure that the Squatter has placed his claims on your finances, your home, your marriage, and your business, but he cannot prevail, so don't allow him to do it. Our God is a God of restoration. If you bring your faith to that next level, God will release to you all that has been stolen from you. He will restore ALL! He is the Great Restorer of families and marriages. Let Him have His way with what is yours.

In the land of the Philistines, this little woman had encountered her Nothing, her place of darkness and void. But out of that same dark space, out of that nothingness, she had regained all. What will you do with your Nothing today?

Elijah's servant had encountered Nothing on six consecutive occasions, but on the seventh, he saw what he was looking for. Rain was coming.

Now another prophet had told this woman to leave her home for seven long years, and in the process it seemed as if she had lost all. But that was not the case. Can you imagine receiving the receipts of seven years' worth of crops all at one time. One moment you're in great need, and the next you are experiencing great abundance. That's how God does it, but He demands that you be faithful in your trials and let them lift you ever higher:

> *When a man's ways please the* LORD*, he maketh even his enemies to be at peace with him.*
>
> Proverbs 16:7

God has declared:

> *The king's heart is in the hand of the* LORD*, as the rivers of water: he turneth it whithersoever he will.*
>
> Proverbs 21:1

God squeezed this king, and out of his heart came the widow's house and lands and payment for all of her losses. Does the enemy really think he's going to steal our money and get away with it? He'd better think again. We are the servants of the Most High God.

God twisted the heart of that king, and out came all that woman's money. Let Him twist hearts for you, so that your blessings can increase. But remember: it is only as our faith is brought to the seventh level, that level of perfection and maturity, that full restoration can come.

You might say, "I don't understand why such restoration has not come to me?" Maybe you gave up at level five. Maybe you didn't persevere long enough to face the king and say, "I want my money." You have to face the king, and you have to say it. Nobody else will do it for you. Satan surely won't give up his claims without a fight.

If you believe for full restoration, and you continue to believe through every coming trial, it will come to you. That's God's promise. Pray, "Lord, restore all," and then be ready to obey whatever He tells you to do. He will surely work for you.

Are you ready? Is your faith strong? Contend for all the fruits, all the benefits, and all the blessings due you.

How strange that this woman went to the place of the Philistines. This name *Philistine* speaks of a place of shame, a place of rolling in the dust. It was shameful for an Israelite to go there. But the word *seven* is more powerful in a positive way than the word *Philistine* is in a negative way.

Early on, this woman made a decree that living in the land of shame would not be her inheritance, and she made an oath daily that she would get back all that she had lost. She was determined not to live the rest of her life in some outer court, covered by shame. She had made this oath to herself. She didn't have to make it to God.

Sometimes I think we miss it, because we think God has to do it all. She made the oath that this would not be her end, that it would not be her inheritance, for she knew that this was not what God had planned for her.

When she finally got the seven-year increase, it was something she did not have to work for, and she did not have to beg for it either. She had made an oath that she was going to get it all back, and she did.

What are you waiting for? Press into *The Seventh Level* and see what God will do for you.

## Chapter 10

# The Preciseness of God's Order

*Now Jericho was straitly shut up because of the children of Israel: none went out, and none came in.*
Joshua 6:1

As we have seen, God wants us to bring our faith to the seventh level, the level of perfection and maturity. He cannot do this for us. He is the Author and the Finisher of our faith, but when we personally bring our faith with our works, by His grace, into a new dimension, that is when we will see the Lord in action. He can only do His work when we have done ours.

Jericho was *"shut up."* This looked like a level of victory for Joshua and his people, but it wasn't the completed victory God had destined for them. Too often we look at situations and say, "Good, my enemies are minding their own business. No one is coming out, and no one is getting in. Let them stay where they are." But that's not right. Those enemies possess some territory that rightfully belongs to you, and you must take it back. This is what God revealed to Joshua:

> *See, I have given into thine hand Jericho, and the king thereof, and the mighty men of valour.*
>
> Joshua 6:2

God wanted Joshua to see what He saw. And what did God see? He saw Jericho, the king of Jericho, and all the mighty men of Jericho in the hands and under the power of the Israelites. So He told Joshua, "I need you to see what I see, through the eyes of faith."

Seeing as God sees will put the spokes in your wheels, and you will suddenly roll on. It will no longer be a problem putting your works with your faith.

God said, *"See I have already given you ..."* That's past tense. It was done. This was not a promise for the future; it was a present reality. It was done. God had already given them the city, He had already given them the king, and He had already given them the mighty men. What a powerful truth!

There were, however, some things the people must do. God now gave them precise instructions:

> *And ye shall compass the city, all ye men of war, and go round about the city once. Thus shalt thou do six days. And seven priests shall bear before the*

*ark seven trumpets of rams' horns: and the seventh day ye shall compass the city seven times, and the priests shall blow with the trumpets. And it shall come to pass, that when they make a long blast with the ram's horn, and when ye hear the sound of the trumpet, all the people shall shout with a great shout; and the wall of the city shall fall down flat, and the people shall ascend up every man straight before him.* Joshua 6:3-5

These instructions were not just for Joshua. They involved all of the people. Each one was to be involved and be involved totally — body, soul, and spirit. Oh, my, how the church needs to get involved today! Nothing will happen if the majority stands back looking on. God did not call us to be cheerleaders. He needs each of us to get into the middle of the ring and get involved in the fight.

Trophies do not come to grandstanders. Trophies come to those who endure to the end and fight the good fight of faith. These are the ones who are right there in the middle of the circle, right there in the middle of the battle. God doesn't need cheerleaders, and He doesn't need grandstanders. Get into the ring and fight, endure, press forward, and take a stand. In other words, put works with your faith.

The seventh level of our faith in never found in the grandstands. It can be experienced only in the ring, in the middle of the fight. Then, all of a sudden things begin to happen, but it involves putting our works with our faith.

Then we must endure to the end, and that means to the end of our trial. The result will be the miraculous — whatever the miraculous consists of in that situation:

> *He that endureth to the end shall be saved, [healed, delivered, made whole, made safe].*
>
> Matthew 10:22

Joshua 6:1 paints a picture of the situation. Jericho was shut up tight. Something was going on. Verse 2 is about how and when faith was imparted to Joshua and his people. That was when God said, *"I have given you the city, its king, and its mighty men."* Verses 3 through 5 consist of the instructions given to them by God about how they were to go about gaining this victory. It involved putting their works with their faith. These instruction were very precise, and they contained a lot of sevens:

> *And SEVEN priests shall bear before the ark SEVEN trumpets of rams' horns: and the SEVENTH day ye shall compass the city SEVEN times, and the priests shall blow with the trumpets.*

These were serious moments, and things had to be done in God's precise timing and in His precise way.

And every single one of the Israelites had to be totally involved in this. They had to be totally committed, just as God is calling us to be totally committed today. We must be totally committed to God and to the action of bringing our faith to the seventh level, so that the victories reserved for us can be fully realized.

God was calling the Israelites, who were just as diverse and different from one another as any other people, to be united and to work together. It was a calling to unity, a coming together to work toward a common goal.

You and I, too, are in this thing together, and we must be totally committed to God and to each other. If not, He will get in our faces and warn us that we are not giving our all. When we are not fully committed to each other, many fall by the wayside.

Far too many people are being led by their emotions. They feel very religious and very churchy, but at the same time, they are often totally out of the will of God for the moment.

As individuals, sin separates us from God. We may appear to be a good person, and we may do the right thing by going to church, but we can still be disobeying God. Even preachers, pastors, apostles, and prophets are sometimes out of the will of God, and it's because they are unwilling to hear the voice of God for this hour and be obedient to it in every way.

When we see a gift being exercised by someone, we think they surely must be doing God's will, but this is often not the case. The spiritual gifts do not belong to individuals; they belong to God. He is looking to the man or woman who is using His gifts to do so for the benefit of the whole Body, but not everyone does that.

Joshua and his people were blessed to be chosen by God to inhabit the Promised Land, but they had to be tested at every stage to see if they were suitable, and the conquest of Jericho was one of the many tests they faced along the way.

The first part of their instructions that day were these: *"And ye shall compass the city, all ye men of war, and go round about the city once. Thus shalt thou do six days"* (Joshua 6:3). This word *compass,* as used here, means "to surround on every side." Every part of going around the city had to be experienced. They could not stop, avoid a certain part, or try to go around a certain situation. They had to experience it all, and they had to do it every day for six days.

In our walk of faith, there are situations, sceneries, people and situations that we come upon that we don't particularly like, but we have to experience them anyway. You have to experience your in-laws and your outlaws. Sometimes you have to experience things about your pastor that you don't like. Can you handle that?

Regardless of what you like or dislike, or who you like or dislike, you are being called upon to *compass* the city, that is to experience every inch of its circumference. Whatever you encounter, you need a made-up mind. You need to declare: "I will endure until the end, and whatever is to be experienced, I will get through it."

The Israelites were to experience every part of the trial, facing the king of Jericho and facing the mighty men of the city. How can you be an overcomer if you don't have something or someone to overcome?

In that moment, God called the Israelites *"men of war."* They may not have felt like *"men of war,"* but that's what He said they were destined to be anyway. He had called the men of Jericho *"mighty men,"* but he called His men *"men of war."* That was what they were about to prove.

This phrase, *men of war*, meant that they stood out as strong and powerful. They were obvious in their might. *Men of war* referred to proven champions. These men were to be feared, whether they knew it or not.

Strong men are not necessarily all champions. Champions know how to *"endure hardness as a good soldier of Jesus Christ"* (2 Timothy 2:3). They have solid and proven testimonies. They've been through the battle, and they endured.

God is calling forth champions today who will stand out above all others. They will not only be strong and prayerful; they will be fully capable of *"do[ing] all things through Christ which strengtheneth [them]"* (Philippians 4:13). These champions are those who always cross the finish line. They do not just talk the talk; they walk the walk. God is again calling for men of war today.

When Joshua heard what God had said, he must have thought to himself, "Jericho has 'mighty men of valour' in it, and they have stood for many years against all who would overrun them. But, on the other hand, if God says that we are *'men of war,'* He is telling us that we are champions. So we will prevail."

Now Joshua set himself to consider carefully the precise instructions God had given. They were to compass the city once a day for seven days, and seven priests were to go before the Ark of the Covenant bearing seven trumpets of rams' horns. These were not the silver trumpets, which were straight. The rams' horns had a curve in them, and because of that curve, these horns made a very different sound. Our victories of faith are often to be won through means considered totally inadequate and utterly foolish in the face of human wisdom. If we, however, in faith, are obedient to God's precepts and to His ways, then He will certainly take those foolish things and use them to confound the mighty.

March around the city once a day for six days. How was that for a battle plan? Then, when it came to the seventh day, they were to march around seven times, with seven priests carrying seven horns. What did it all mean? To the Israelites, the number seven was the symbolic seal of their national covenant with God, and because of that, it was a sacred number. It was, in fact, the most sacred number. Their God was perfect and His work was perfect. If He said carry rams' horns, then through the foolishness of those rams' horns the enemy would be defeated.

Paul later wrote to the Corinthian believers:

> *(For the weapons of our warfare are not carnal, but mighty through God to the pulling down of strong holds;) casting down imaginations, and every high thing that exalteth itself against the knowledge of God, and bringing into captivity every thought to the obedience of Christ; and having in a readiness to revenge all disobedience, when your obedience is fulfilled.*
>
> 2 Corinthians 10:4-6

When he said, *"the weapons of our warfare are not carnal,"* he was comparing them to what seemed useful and powerful to the carnal eye. Spiritual weapons do not appear mighty, but God has always used simple things to bring victory to His people.

The use of something simple does not diminish God. In fact, when He uses the simple to produce great miracles, it reveals Him as Almighty as nothing else can. Out of simplicity God produces greatness, and that glorifies Him and lifts Him up. Miracles happen because our weapons, although they appear useless to the natural eye, are actually *"mighty through God to the pulling down of strong holds."*

Joshua was very familiar with the strength and notoriety of Jericho. It was a walled and protected city, in the natural, a stronghold. But God had given him the secret to its overthrow: marching seven days, with seven priests holding seven rams' horns. Surely God was about to reveal His power again through the simple.

Joshua was not worried. There was power and preciseness in the number seven, and it was sacred or holy. It meant that God had a covenant with His people, and He would use the seven priests with their seven trumpets during seven days to give them victory. Joshua was so sure of it that he called his men together and shared these insights with them.

But just because God had called them *"men of war"* didn't mean that they had arrived. They now had to respond to what God was saying, take their faith to a new level, and put works with their words. God had shown them what they could do, but now it was up to them to do it. They clearly needed to move up to another level, to maturity and perfection.

Which of us no longer needs polishing? If these men were already *"men of war"* (champions) then they were about to become greater men of war (greater champions). Without the physical to rely on, they would need to trust God as never before, they would have to perfect their confidence in Him, and their obedience would now have to be tested to the max.

God had already done them the favor of describing the scene of victory He had planned:

> *And it shall come to pass, that when they make a long blast with the ram's horn, and when ye hear the sound of the trumpet, all the people shall shout with a great shout; and the wall of the city shall fall down flat, and the people shall ascend up every man straight before him.* Joshua 6:5

Jericho was theirs for the taking.

There is one element of this victory at Jericho that we have not yet discussed. The priests had to be in this march, and the men of war had to be in this march, but there was another essential element to victory. They must not go out without the Ark of the Covenant accompanying them.

The Ark, of course, represented the very presence of God. When you get on your journey of faith, and you know that something has to come down, walls have to fall, you'd better have something with you more than your personal faith. You cannot march successfully without the presence of God accompanying you. So you'd better learn to honor God and have a love and appreciation for His presence.

When you journey with God as your Companion, and you honor His presence and give Him glory, you are destined for a successful and prosperous trip, no matter what enemy tries to stop you. Joshua and his people were carriers of God's presence, and you must be too.

It would be scary to face the trials of life without the presence of God. In every crisis, we want Him near. Therefore His presence must be honored, supported, and recognized.

We also need to enjoy the presence of God. Take Him with you wherever you go. May our lives be less and less about us and more and more about Him.

So there were to be seven priests, seven trumpets of rams' horn, seven days, and seven times on the seventh day. They couldn't lose if they obeyed God in this way.

The seventh level, where your faith must be brought, is a special level designed by God Himself. Don't despise it, and don't neglect it.

At times you will experience that dark Nothing area. When the people of Israel were marching around the walls of Jericho on day one, day two, and day three, it seemed dark. Their prospects seemed dark. Day five and day six did not improve in this regard. Even when they had marched around the third time on the seventh day, things still looked dark. I imagine that when they marched around the sixth time on the seventh day, that had to be the darkest hour. They had done all of that, and still there was no visible change — nothing. But never forget: the darkest time is right before the dawn, and that is the most special time because you are passing every obstacle, and the supernatural is about to come into focus.

Maturity is about to materialize. The less-than-perfect is about to reach perfection. The better is about to become the best. The great is about to become the greater. Your faith is about to turn to faithfulness. You have known the Author of your faith, but now you will know the Finisher. You have met the Originator, but now you will know the Perfecter. Your Nothing is about to become Something, and your darkness is about to become light.

This is what happens at the seventh level. It is a very special time. Sadly, some have already fallen by the wayside in the previous rounds. They were deceived about what to expect, so they got trapped, and fell. But not Joshua. He was ready for the next level, and he called the people to get ready too.

How about you? Are you ready to press toward *The Seventh Level*?

## Chapter 11

# The Last Push to Victory

*And it came to pass on the seventh day, that they rose early about the dawning of the day, and compassed the city after the same manner seven times: only on that day they compassed the city seven times. And it came to pass at the seventh time, when the priests blew with the trumpets, Joshua said unto the people, Shout; for the Lord hath given you the city.*

Joshua 6:15-16

Early on that first morning, Joshua made sure that everyone was up and ready. They had a journey to make. They had some impossibilities to accomplish. And so they set out. The same was true for the second day, the third, the fourth, the fifth, and the sixth. On those days, the orders were a little different:

*And Joshua had commanded the people, saying, Ye shall not shout, nor make any noise with your voice,*

> *neither shall any word proceed out of your mouth, until the day I bid you shout; then shall ye shout.*
> Joshua 6:10

There was a specific process to follow. God had said they would march around in this way for six days, and then they would move to the seventh level, and things would be done differently, and everything had to be done in the prescribed order. Even men of war need order, especially men of war.

These men were not to act until Joshua gave the order. This was not every man doing his own thing. This was the army of the Lord in unity of purpose obeying the commands He passed to them through His servant Joshua. Joshua was the commander on the ground under the Great Commander, and so obedience to Joshua was obedience to God.

People can be so easily deceived when too many are trying to give orders. The result is that those orders are conflicting, and the people don't know which way to go or what exactly to do. This shows that the orders did not come from God. When God speaks, we know what to do. His orders are clear and certain. Fortunately, the people obeyed that day:

> *So the ark of the LORD compassed the city, going about it once: and they came into the camp, and lodged in the camp.* Joshua 6:11

The first day had ended. Nothing appeared to be happening, but it didn't matter because this was a march of faith, not of sight. This same routine continued during the coming days, and the result was more or less the same. Nothing happened. But Joshua was not discouraged. He knew that the most important day was yet to come. If they could persevere until the end of the seventh day, victory would be theirs.

That day finally came, as it will for you:

> *And it came to pass on the seventh day, that they rose early about the dawning of the day, and compassed the city after the same manner seven times: only on that day they compassed the city seven times. And it came to pass at the seventh time, when the priests blew with the trumpets, Joshua said unto the people, Shout; for the LORD hath given you the city.*
>
> Joshua 6:15-16

*"And it came to pass at the seventh time ..."* It came to pass. This is one of the most powerful phrases in the Bible. God had promised it, and it came to pass. It didn't come to pass on the first day or the fifth, and it didn't come to pass when the children of Israel woke up on the seventh day. It came to pass at a precise moment, in a precise place, and in a precise situation. It came to pass when the people had fully obeyed God. It came to pass when they

had pressed beyond their doubts and fears and reached the seventh level, and it came to pass when they all shouted as one.

Joshua had told them to hold their peace until that moment, and they had. Then, when he gave the order, they all shouted at once. Was that so important? Absolutely! God wants to teach us order, the order of faith, the order of carrying out what He has told us to do. God performs His mighty acts when we have done our part in faith, and then when we shout in faith, it becomes a reality. It comes to pass.

The sounding of the rams' horns was also part of this mix:

> *So the people shouted when the priests blew with the trumpets: and it came to pass, when the people heard the sound of the trumpet, and the people shouted with a great shout, that the wall fell down flat, so that the people went up into the city, every man straight before him, and they took the city.* Joshua 6:20

These trumpets, again, were rams' horns, and the traditional use of the rams' horns was to sound the beginning of the year of Jubilee. What the Jewish people called the year of Jubilee was celebrated at the end of seven cycles of seven years, and many wonderful things were destined to take place. Debts were canceled, and slaves were freed. It was a joyous time of celebration for all.

Some, no doubt, wanted to sound Jubilee after the first day of marching, but that was premature. They had a long way to go yet. They had not proven their faithfulness yet. They had not passed the test yet. The sounding for Jubilee was for a prescribed moment, and that moment was when they had reached the seventh level, not one second before.

Some people are showy, and so they try to jump the gun. They want to cross the finish line and win the prize without ever having run the race. They want to sound Jubilee when they are only halfway around the city on the third day. They need to settle their spirits and get in order. There is a right way and a wrong way to do things, and when the right thing is done in the wrong way, the result is the same. Nothing happens.

If you have faith, don't worry about showing it to others. Keep on doing what you are commissioned to do, and in time people will see your faith. Do things in order, in a balanced way, with preciseness, and step-by-step bring your faith to the seventh level. Then we can all shout together.

When the trumpets were blown at the prescribed moment and the people shouted as one, suddenly something began to happen. Those walls came down, and your walls will come down too, as you learn to be faithful and to operate in order.

It's time to get with the program. We will not take our Jerichos individually. We have to do this thing together, in oneness, in holy cooperation. We need to pray and intercede together, we need to stand together, we need to believe together, we need to preach and teach together, and we need to carry out our vision and our mandate together.

The reason rams' horns were used as trumpets by the people of Israel is that they sounded clear and precise notes. They were perfectly pitched. That's what we need today. We have too many confusing sounds around us. Let a clear note be sounded.

Until our faith can send forth a jubilant, but clear sound, nothing will happen. Just because we can speak in tongues does not mean that we are sending forth a clear sound. Clarity is one of the greatest needs of our day — clarity of vision, clarity of declarations and clarity of process. Until we all understand what our goal is and what it is that we each must do to achieve that goal, we can do little.

The faith of Joshua and his men and their resulting works, their actions, their obedience to the call of faith, suddenly began to put stress on that sacred number seven. Their faith was evident, and the preciseness of their order in response to that faith was blameless ... until that sacred number seven had to say, "I can't take anymore. I have to break out, I have to break through, and I have to break in with victory." When the sacred number seven is honored, the supernatural always happens. God always moves. He works because of our works.

*"The people shouted with a great shout."* This was a joyful sound, and it signified the moment the people broke through to that seventh level. As a result, the wall could no longer stand. It *"fell down flat."* That was an incredible moment in time.

Perhaps some thought it would never come, but they kept pressing forward, doing what they knew to do, what they had been commanded to do. They did not necessarily feel great joy in doing it, but they were faithful and persevered. Then, suddenly, they had broken through to the other side, and no barrier could stand before them. Their faith had risen with each new day of test, until they had reached the seventh level, and the wellspring of joy sprung up within them, and they shouted joyfully.

Joy is a powerful force, and when it flows, it creates an amazing sound. The trumpeters did their part, but then each of the men of war joined in, and it must have been a deafening chorus. These people knew in that moment that their faith had broken through. They knew they had touched Heaven, and their shout reflected that fact.

This must have been terrifying for the hapless residents of Jericho. It was easy to see that the faith of the men of Israel had reached the seventh level. It had been perfected. It was mature. It was truly sanctified, and this produced a pure, deep, genuine, and unmistakable shout of joy. Wow!

My friend, you will not have joyful faith until you get to the seventh level. Your faith, when perfected and matured, will put stress on the number seven, and you, too, will break through into victory and genuine joy.

Trials come and trials go, but if we press on in faith, eventually we will arrive at the seventh level, and suddenly we will be filled with shouts of joy that cannot be contained. Our God longs to hear this type of genuine shout of joy arising from His Church, and when He hears it, He will respond and remove every obstacle from our path to conquest.

So, if you want real joy, then stick it out and keep on sticking it out until your victory comes. Stay in the race, and don't get distracted, and you will eventually reach the finish line and gain your prize.

Genuine shouts of joy brought the walls of Jericho down, and joy will do the same for you. I can imagine it was the first time those walls had heard shouts like those. What a joyful sound!

Jesus said, *"He that endureth to the end shall be saved"* (Matthew 10:22). The same is true for healing, deliverance, and prosperity. Always remember the scriptural admonition:

> *Not by might, nor by power, but by my spirit, saith the LORD of hosts.* Zechariah 4:6

It is God's Spirit working in us and through us, in His order and with His specific and precise instructions, that brings us victory. Yes, He is the Author and Finisher of our faith, but we each have our precise and important part to play.

May God free us of any and all religious spirits that would divert us from our specific goals, and may we, as God's beloved Church, begin to bring forth a more certain sound for battle.

So, what are you waiting for? Press on the *The Seventh Level.*

## Chapter 12

# Humility and the Seventh Level

*Now Naaman, captain of the host of the king of Syria, was a great man with his master, and honourable, because by him the* Lord *had given deliverance unto Syria: he was also a mighty man in valour, but he was a leper.* 2 Kings 5:1

Before moving on, let us review once again: God desires that we bring our faith to a higher level of perfection and maturity. There is a journey, a process of taking our faith from level to level to level, until it gets to that seventh level, and then the supernatural happens.

We started with the truth: *"Now faith is the substance of things hoped for, the evidence of things not seen"* (Hebrews 11:1). We have discovered that Jesus is the Author and the Finisher, or the Originator and the Perfecter of our faith. And I asked the question early on: what do you do when there is Nothing?

Elijah told his servant to go and look toward the sea and to come back and report what he had seen. The little guy came back with the report of *"nothing."* What do we do when there is *"nothing"*? Well, as we are learning, you continue to do what you started doing in the beginning. That's exactly what you do. Why give up? Why quit? Why turn back before you have reached your goal? Don't stop now. Nothing cannot hinder you, for God is in that Nothing.

Like the prophet's servant, you must go again as many times as you need to ... until you have brought your faith to that seventh level and something happens. Then, suddenly, out of your Nothing comes Something, because in that Nothing there was always Something. In Nothing, Something is just waiting to emerge.

What good news it is that God is the omnipresent God, everywhere at the same time! This means that He is in our nothingness. It doesn't matter what color Nothing may be: black, red, pink, or purple. It may all look like Nothing, but God is in it. He is just waiting to manifest Himself, and He *will* manifest Himself when you are determined to take yourself to that seventh level of faith and obedience, that level of breaking through the nothingness of your situation into the Somethingness of God's promise.

With that as a background, let us now look at the biblical story of Naaman. We don't know a lot about

Naaman, but what we do know is significant. We know that this man was *"captain of the host of the king of Syria,"* was *"a great man with his master,"* was *"honourable,"* and was a hero of sorts *"because by him the* LORD *had given deliverance unto Syria."* We know that *"he was also a mighty man in valour,"* and we know that despite all of that greatness, *"he was a leper."* Today that word *leper* still inspires fear, but in Naaman's day, it was much more so. Leprosy was a death sentence, and if a person with leprosy lived, they did so as an outcast. Why would God allow something so terrible to happen to such a fine and respected man?

The answer is simply that God chooses the mode of testing He will use to perfect our faith. He not only chooses the mode; He also chooses the length and severity of each test. And there is no one-rule-fits-all with God. He knows each of us, and He shapes our individual tests to meet our particular need. We are not all tested the same, for we are not all on the same spiritual level. God knows best in every test. We must trust Him.

You have no vote in this. You have no choice in the matter. This is God's decision. You just do what you are called on to do by faith — or you fail the test. When you are tested, you can fall into despondency, sure that God has allowed a curse to fall upon you, or you can exercise some spiritual discernment and recognize and be willing to accept the fact that God has laid out a particular test for you as an individual. He has the right to do that, and His love demands it.

If you have accepted Jesus as your personal Savior, then God lives in you. And that God who lives in you will put your faith to regular tests, to determine if you will be faithful or not. Some of us do well when everything seems to be going our way, but when tests come, we easily become discouraged.

But facing a test is nothing to be discouraged about. God has invested a lot in you, and He has a right to test you periodically. Accept that fact, and prepare yourself to withstand every test.

Naaman was an army captain, he was a great man, and he was an honorable man. This meant that he was very wealthy.

He was also a mighty man, a skilled soldier, but he had a most serious problem: he was a leper. Leprosy was so contagious and so deadly that Old Testament Law forced lepers to separate themselves from the rest of society and live elsewhere, wherever they could. The king of Syria had favored Naaman and allowed him to continue in society because he was a man of great wealth, great strength, great knowledge, and great experience.

Naaman was mighty, very forceful, and effective in all that he did, and that's why the king had elevated him to the position of captain of his hosts. Naaman had a lot going for him in life, but he also had this one deadly threat that could cut his career and his life short. He had a serious test to overcome.

There also existed, in the heart of this leper, a hunger for the true God, and one day a seed of faith was planted there that caused him to make a journey in search of God and His healing power. It happened in an unusual way (as God often does things).

Recently the Syrians had led some forays into Israeli territory and had taken captive some Israelites and brought them back as slaves. One of them, *"a little maid,"* was now serving in Naaman's home (2 Kings 5:2). That little maid was a woman of faith, and she testified to her mistress:

> *And she said unto her mistress, Would God my lord were with the prophet that is in Samaria! for he would recover him of his leprosy.*
>
> 2 Kings 5:3

Instead of being immediately and easily dismissed, this news was received and repeated, and it soon reached Naaman's ears. He, too, was touched by it, and as soon as he could, he sought permission from his king to go and see if he could find the prophet the maid had mentioned. Amazingly, the Syrian king actually encouraged Naaman to take this journey and even said that he would send a letter of introduction to be hand-carried to the king of Israel on his behalf.

Encouraged, Naaman loaded his pack animals with treasures (to pay out as needed), got in his chariot, and set out for Israel.

When Naaman arrived and presented his letter to the king of Israel, the king was dismayed by it. Who could believe that he had power to heal leprosy? He didn't have healing power. He thought it must be a plot to accuse him and do him harm. Was someone trying to start a war with him?

Fortunately, Elisha, *"the man of God,"* heard about this and sent a message to the king:

> *And it was so, when Elisha the man of God had heard that the king of Israel had rent his clothes, that he sent to the king, saying, Wherefore hast thou rent thy clothes? let him come now to me, and he shall know that there is a prophet in Israel.* 2 Kings 5:8

Real prophets are bold and brassy. They know what they know, they know what they can do, and they don't mind speaking it out loud, because God has called them to be His spokespersons. There is something about prophets that is always challenging to the people they meet: *"Let him come now to me, and he shall know that there is a prophet in Israel."* Wow!

This prophet meant business. He wanted the Syrians to have a testimony of who God was, and he sensed that God was using him to give them this opportunity.

The king had not welcomed this challenge. This wasn't his responsibility. He had no healing ministry. The request from the king of Syria only embarrassed and upset him. He worried that he might have a fight on his hands. But the prophet had no such fears. He welcomed this challenge and recognized it for what it was, an opportunity to reveal the greatness of the God of Israel and to win others to His side. *"Send him to me!"* He boldly proclaimed.

This was not spiritual pride. The man knew his calling. When you know that you know who you are, and you know that you know what you can do, it makes your extraordinarily bold. Soon Naaman, with his whole entourage, was standing outside Elisha's door:

> *So Naaman came with his horses and with his chariot, and stood at the door of the house of Elisha.*
>
> 2 Kings 5:9

Naaman must have had very conflicting feelings. He was a mighty man, a captain, and a trusted servant of the king, and that must have been very personally satisfying and very personally rewarding. In one sense, he was a very proud man. But, at the same time, he could not deny that he had leprosy, and it was a hideous sickness, slowly disfiguring the body and destroying its extremities. This caused lepers to be shunned and misunderstood.

Because he was captain of the armies of Syria, we can be sure that Naaman was not slouchily dressed. His chariot was immaculate, and he had the finest horses. He had servants who handled the pack animals, drove the chariot for him, and otherwise attended to his every need. He was someone to be reckoned with, captain of the host of Syria, handpicked by his master. So, we might say, Naaman was a big wheel, a big shot, and he was accustomed to being treated with deference. He might be a leper, but he was still an important man.

Each of us faces unique tests, and some of them are easier than others. If we had it our way, we would cruise on in to the finish line with ease, but there is no guarantee of that. Only God knows what it will take to get you to the seventh level. Trust Him that what He chooses to put you through is exactly what you need at the moment. That is why He has required it.

When you are first faced with a trial, you have no way of understanding exactly what is happening. All you know is that you suddenly have a need. It will surely seem that the enemy has been given a free hand to assault you. One of the things you can be sure of in that moment is that God is up to something good. As a believer in Christ, you can be sure that every moment of your life and every step on your spiritual journey is of vital importance. Nothing happens by chance or without reason. God is in control of your present and your future.

Naaman's faith was being tested, his obedience was being tested, and his humility was being tested. All three of these elements had to be brought to the seventh level.

Naaman had it in his heart to show proper respect for God and His prophet, but it also appears that he intended to use the force of his position and, if needed, his treasures, to put pressure on the man of God.

When Elisha was made aware of the presence of the captain at his door, the man was standing there in all of his ceremonial regalia. His chariots and horses were at their best, and his servants had donned their best outfits, all meant to impress. But Elisha was not impressed, and he declined to appear and speak with the Syrian. Was this rudeness on his part? Was it some sort of racial slight?

Because Elisha was a prophet of God we must conclude that his reaction was part of God's answer to Naaman. He wanted this man to know that all of the regalia in the world does not impress Him in the least.

To Naaman, his appearance was of political and military significance, but far too many times we try to impress God with our religious regalia. And He cannot be impressed in this way. Our demonstrations of showiness just serve to turn God off, and, in the end, we must bow in humility and recognize His greatness — if we are to receive anything meaningful at His hand.

Even good things can sometimes become a source of religious pride for us. We may think, for example, that God should be impressed with how much we speak in tongues. He's not. We may think that He should be impressed with how much we give. He's not. When you have a need and you approach God for His help, you have one alternative and only one. It was expressed by Peter in his first letter to the churches:

> *Be clothed with humility: for God resisteth the proud, and giveth grace to the humble. Humble yourselves therefore under the mighty hand of God, that he may exalt you in due time: casting all your care upon him; for he careth for you.* 1 Peter 5:5-7

God requires humility.

Having been faithful in the past and having proven yourself in some great test is no substitute for current humility and obedience. If overcoming spiritual tests has filled you with spiritual pride, that pride will now have to be dealt with before you can go higher.

With regard to today's test, it doesn't matter how many times in the past you have proven your faith by your obedience. Maybe you were very humble when those trials came to you years ago, but what counts is the here and now. What is the condition of your heart right now, today, this very minute?

The way you approach God means everything to Him and will determine the outcome of your trial. If you approach Him in the correct way, with the correct spirit, His heart is touched, and you will have your answer. If not, the opposite is true.

In this, Naaman made a terrible mistake. He seriously overestimated the importance of his position in God's eyes, and he had to learn humility before he could be healed. This is a mistake we all make at some point. Never forget: God is everything, and we are nothing.

Yes, He has done wonders in you and for you. Yes, He has placed a special calling upon your life. And there is much more for you to be thankful for. But, whatever you do, don't let anything that God does for you exalt the self. God must receive all the glory, and if we fail to learn this lesson, we will never reach the seventh level. Self must be crucified, daily if necessary.

Naaman's first mistake was this approach of formality. He clearly wanted to impress, and God was clearly not impressed. I'm sure that you feel like me sometimes. When I see how people try to put on a religious show, it makes me want to throw up. I can't imagine how it must make God feel.

God's healing is never dispensed because we somehow deserve it. It only comes by His grace, because He loves us so. And it grieves the Holy Ghost when we try to impress the Creator of the Universe with our worthiness.

God's miracles come to those who open their hearts to Him, not to those who somehow deserve miracles because of their good works. God's financial blessings never come because we have proved our worthiness. They come because we recognize His greatness, not our own.

Word came to Elisha that this powerful foreigner *"stood at the door"* (2 Kings 5:9). This word *stood,* as it is used here, means "to confirm." By taking his ceremonial stance at the door, Naaman was attempting to confirm his social importance, and he expected the prophet to confirm him, as well. As he stood at the door, he was sending a message to Elisha. "I am waiting for you to confirm who I am and what I will receive from your God."

Some of us might have been impressed with that presentation, but you can't fool a real prophet of God. That is, you can't fool the God who is in the prophet. Elisha knew what was going on even before he was advised by his servants, and he knew how very foolish such displays of pride are.

Naaman had leprosy and was doomed to die, and yet he was more concerned with looking good than he was with making sure his spirit was right. What a pitiful sight! A man tying to prove his importance, when God wanted him to recognize his nothingness. The prophet, therefore, was led to respond in the opposite way as Naaman expected. He refused to go out to personally receive the man. Instead, he sent a servant with a message:

> *And Elisha sent a messenger unto him, saying, Go and wash in Jordan seven times, and thy flesh shall come again to thee, and thou shalt be clean.*
>
> 2 Kings 5:10

Wow! That sounds good to me. Naaman would be healed (and that had been his goal for the beginning). So God was answering His prayer and meeting His need. Why, then, was Naaman so angry?

> *But Naaman was wroth, and went away, and said, Behold, I thought, He will surely come out to me, and stand, and call on the name of the LORD his God, and strike his hand over the place, and recover the leper. Are not Abana and Pharpar, rivers of Damascus, better than all the waters of Israel? may I not wash in them, and be clean? So he turned and went away in a rage.* 2 Kings 5:11-12

God had heard the cry of the Syrian's heart and shown him how to be healed, but he *"was wroth,"* and he *"turned and went away in a rage."* Wow! How sad is that?

Healing was within his reach, but because he felt offended that the prophet had not done this thing in the ceremonial way he had expected, he was going to walk away empty handed.

So why didn't Elisha go to the door to meet the man and show him the normal respect? Why did he refuse to go out, after the man had traveled so far, and, instead, sent a servant to bring him a message (another apparent affront)? It was because God hates pride and could not honor pride with His blessings. Pride will inherit nothing! Humility will inherit all!

Some people are saved and speak in tongues, but they will never get anywhere with God because of their stinking pride. Some are faithful tithers and givers, but their pride prevents them from moving into God's fullness for their lives. God is not impressed with your ability to speak in tongues or any other gift that He has graciously manifested in your life. He is not impressed with you returning to Him a small portion of what He has blessed you with. If you can't get rid of that awful pride, you will never reach the seventh level.

Part of Naaman's anger was about the fact that the prophet had not confirmed his importance, but another part of it was about the message the servant had delivered:

## Humility and the Seventh Level

*Go and wash in Jordan seven times, and thy flesh shall come again to thee, and thou shalt be clean.*

2 Kings 5:10

The message to the man of pride was one of humility. He must go down to the Jordan River, and he must dip himself in it seven times. If he was willing to do that, he would be marvelously healed. He was not willing.

God knows just how to deal with each of us, and what He tells us will be tailored for our spiritual need, just as this message was especially tailored for Naaman. God deals with us on our particular spiritual level, and we must respond. But this message of humility is for every man and every woman of every nation and every level of maturity.

God knows what is best. Even though His plan is so very different from our own, we must always have a humble approach to Him. He has a miracle, a healing, or an answer waiting for us, but we must always recognize that He is the Giver, and we are the receivers. If we, as receivers, have not yet received, it may very well be that our steps are not ordered right. Go back to His feet and start over. Don't ever think that you are so big and so spiritual that you can move to the head. He is the Head; our place is always at His feet.

In spite of everything, Elisha provided Captain Naaman with a revelation of the seventh level. If he was willing to humble himself seven times, he would be healed.

As a Syrian, Naaman could not have known the meaning of the number seven to the ancient Israelites. He didn't know that it represented perfection or completion to them and had to do with their covenant with God. It also represented a full step up, arriving at the goal or mark, but he didn't have to know that to be blessed by it. He now had his chance at a new life.

We can't stop at the sixth level, the level of man, and expect to accomplish anything great. The seventh level is God's level, the place of full obedience to Him. Something always happens when we go there. It is the realm of supernatural experience.

Elisha had said that Naaman must dip seven times, and that signified God's order. He had to do God's will, not his own, as important as he was in the natural. He needed to get something straight in his spirit. God's mandate to him was: "submit or split," and for a while it looked as if he would surely split. But as we have noted, if you choose to split, then you will be the loser. Enduring to the end brings the promise of salvation, healing, and deliverance. Quitters forfeit all rights and privileges.

The challenge to the seventh level was a very real test of Naaman's willingness to bring his faith and obedience and his meekness and humility before God, to the level of fruition.

His first response was anger: *"But Naaman was wroth, and went away ..."* (verse 11), *"So he turned and went away in a rage"* (verse 12). #1). He was angry over a perceived personal slight on the part of the prophet. #2). He was angry because the prophet had not done things the way he imagined they should be done, and #3). He was angry over the suggestion that he could be healed by washing in the Jordan river:

> *Are not Abana and Pharpar, rivers of Damascus, better than all the waters of Israel? may I not wash in them, and be clean?* 2 Kings 5:12

Even in those days, the Jordan had a reputation as a dirty river. Other rivers were clearly better, so why should he have to wash in the muddy Jordan? The two rivers Naaman named as more suitable alternatives, *Abana and Pharpar,* were such clear rushing streams that they produced superb drinking water that was much sought after. They were like fountains, and they were well known to Naaman as the best rivers in Damascus. Surely these were preferable to all the waters of Israel.

Naaman knew the Jordan and knew it was nothing like the Abana and the Pharpar. I can concur. I have seen the Jordan River, and I was not impressed with it either. But this was all about obedience, not about the quality of the river water. God does what He has to do to deal with our arrogance. Haughtiness, arrogance and egotistical spirits and attitudes will hinder any person who seeks God, even the best of Christians. And even though we always think we have a better way than God, this will be done His way and in His time or not at all.

Elisha had told Naaman to go and dip in the Jordan seven times, and the promise was that he would be healed. That should have been enough, but Naaman began to reason away the importance of that word. This kind of reasoning produces murmuring, complaining, and questioning.

Murmuring and complaining usually focus on outward circumstances, the convenience or inconvenience to the flesh. Please notice that man's reasonings have no regard for God or His words. That was why God said through Isaiah:

> *Come now, and let us reason together, saith the* *Lord.* Isaiah 1:18

Reasoning in cooperation with God can produce eternal results, but anytime we reason apart from God and His Word, we are in trouble. *Reasoning* means "to consider both sides; look at both sides." What's right and what's wrong. What's God and what's the devil? What's God and what's me? There is nothing wrong with reasoning, but you have to get God into the equation, or your reasoning will always lead you to a wrong conclusion.

God has given us soul power, or reasoning ability, but He insists that we do it in cooperation with Him. If we get into His Word and reason with Him, the result is always supernatural. The supernatural comes forth by the Word, and out from the Word. God has spoken it, and when we act upon it, then the Spirit kicks in and produces the miraculous. Our own reasoning produces failure.

We hear the Word, and when we agree with it, the Spirit kicks in. We hear the Word, get the Word in us, act upon the Word, and then the Spirit does its part. But when we reason in our own resources or understanding, God will just stand there looking at us and not get involved at all. By our attitude, we are showing that we don't think we really need Him.

Naaman had his own plan. He expected to be treated with great ceremony. Instead of humbling himself before the Lord's prophet, he actually expected the prophet of the Lord to come humbly before him.

When Naaman said, *"I thought,"* what was it that he was thinking? He thought surely the prophet would come out and stand and confirm him ceremonially, recognizing his title and his authority. But why would a man who was a leper have such pride and arrogance? And why would a person with such a serious need approach a prophet of God in this way? That ego of his had to go. He had a death sentence hanging over him, and it was no time to stand on ceremony.

Naaman seriously overestimated his importance. He overestimated himself. The self always does that.

God was dealing with Naaman about humility, and Naaman wanted to argue about which river had better bathing properties. The rivers in Syria were clear and beautiful, and he was already imagining himself there doing some dipping, but God had other ideas. He declares:

> *For my thoughts are not your thoughts, neither are your ways my ways, saith the* Lord. *For as the heavens are higher than the earth, so are my ways higher than your ways, and my thoughts than your thoughts.* Isaiah 55:8-9

> *For after that in the wisdom of God the world by wisdom knew not God, it pleased God by the foolishness of preaching to save them that believe. For the Jews require a sign, and the Greeks seek after wisdom: but we preach Christ crucified, unto the Jews a stumblingblock, and unto the Greeks foolishness; but unto them which are called, both Jews and Greeks, Christ the power of God, and the wisdom of God. Because the foolishness of God is wiser than men; and the weakness of God is stronger than men.* 1 Corinthians 1:21-25

*But the natural man receiveth not the things of the Spirit of God; for they are foolishness unto him; neither can he know them, because they are spiritually discerned. But he that is spiritual judgeth all things, yet he himself is judged of no man. For who hath known the mind of the Lord, that he may instruct Him? But we have the mind of Christ.*
1 Corinthians 2:14-16

*Let no man deceive himself. If any man among you seemeth to be wise in this world, let him become a fool, that he may be wise. For the wisdom of this world is foolishness with God. For it is written, He taketh the wise in their own craftiness. And again, The Lord knoweth the thoughts of the wise, that they are vain.* 1 Corinthians 3:18-20

*Be not wise in thine own eyes ... .* Proverbs 3:7

*Only by pride cometh contention; but with the well advised is wisdom.* Proverbs 13:10

When we are in a very serious trial, we need a miracle. We need an answer from God. We need the supernatural. But if we don't conquer pride, arrogance, and ego, if we don't conquer self, there is nothing that God can do for us.

Have you noticed how contentious prideful people get? They cannot ever receive from God until their pride has been dealt a deathblow.

Naaman had grown accustomed to his pomp and circumstance, and, being a man of authority, he thought he knew best how things should be done. Human wisdom is always puffed up.

Fortunately, Naaman was saved by some good and faithful servants who came to him now and pointed out to him that, in his insistence that things be done his way, he was about to miss the miracle he so desperately needed:

> *And his servants came near, and spake unto him, and said, My father, if the prophet had bid thee do some great thing, wouldest thou not have done it? How much rather then, when he saith to thee, wash, and be clean?* 2 Kings 5:13

Thank God that we have some friends, some intercessors, some fellow believers who have more than just common sense; they have God in them. They have humility, and because they love you, they will tell you, "Wait! You're about to miss your miracle."

Naaman's faithful servants said to him, "Let's reason this thing out." They had heard the promise of the Word of God, and it sounded very good to them. They were clinging to that promise. Thank God for those who cling to His Word and then come to encourage us to obey Him.

The testings of self were so strong in Naaman that they nearly caused him to miss his miracle. But when he actually thought about it, he realized that his servants were absolutely right. The prophet had not asked him to do something difficult. In fact, what he required was very simple, and he hadn't asked for any of the treasures Naaman carried. Why, then, had he been so arrogant? He suddenly saw the light of it.

We know Naaman's name today, but we don't even know the names of those servants who saved his life. They are known in Heaven, however, for they had true judgement.

Now Naaman was ready to obey:

> *Then went he down, and dipped himself seven times in Jordan, according to the saying of the man of God: and his flesh came again like unto the flesh of a little child, and he was clean.* 2 Kings 5:14

*"Then went he down."* In a moment of time, conviction hit the man. In a moment of time, something struck his spirit. He had found the prophet he was seeking, and the man was a genuine prophet of God. He had not asked for money or sought anything for himself. And the most important thing was that he

had promised the needed healing: *"Thy flesh shall come again to thee, and thou shalt be clean"* (Verse 10). As he thought on all of this, faith began to rise up within him, and a desire for obedience began to squirm within him. I can't say for sure how long Naaman had to deal with this struggle between his faith and his obedience and his pride issue. The important thing is that he eventually was moved to do the right thing. In a moment of time, he made an about-face. He overruled the flesh, and decided to do things God's way. On his journey home, he would have to pass the Jordan, but he was now willing to submit to its waters.

We can imagine that he was perhaps tempted to rush back home where he was so loved and honored, but whatever temptations he had to face, he overcame them all because he went and dipped in the Jordan.

This was his private and personal test. The prophet was not there to see him. His pastor was not there to check on him and make sure he did what he needed to do. He had to face Jordan by himself, and so do you.

*"Then went he down, and dipped himself."* He did it!

The first time Naaman dipped in the Jordan, he must have been thinking, "This water is just as muddy as I remembered it. I look like a different man with all this mud on me, but I can tell that I'm not healed yet."

I imagine that about then his pride had another talk with him. This wasn't working. His original idea had been better. He was foolish to do this. He should just go home and find some other way to be healed.

Naaman had to have a little talk with his pride that day. He said, "Pride, I'm going to baptize you today," and he went down for the second time.

When he came up the second time, the third time, and the fourth time, there didn't seem to be any change. His skin was the same. But three or four times was not enough. He had been told that he had to bring his faith (and his humility) to the seventh level. He had to finally conquer self.

Sometimes, when we are in a long trial, it almost seems that self waits patiently for a time. Then, toward the end of the trial, when you are about to break through into victory, old self raises his ugly head and you have to conquer him once again.

Refuse to listen to self. Put that flesh down. Crucify it. Baptize it. And then keep moving on up until you have come to the seventh level. Know that you are about to experience the supernatural. Grit your teeth and have some old fashioned tenacity. Once you have experienced that sudden change of heart and mind, then press on until victory comes. Don't let anything hold you back from your victory, your healing.

You have to submerge self and not just for a moment. Keep him there, and don't let him come up for air until he is dead. Submerge self into the unknown, into the world of nothing. It's a type of baptism. All of the old must go under and be buried. Deal with self and pride totally and for all time. Self is prideful, arrogant, self-righteousness, and haughty, and this spirit must be put out of the church if we are to have God's blessings in these last days.

*"Then went he down, and dipped himself seven times."* When he was about to go down that seventh time, Naaman must have been wondering, "What will people back home think of me? Will I still be their captain, that mighty and honorable man they looked up to?" Then he decided, "Who cares?" And he plunged beneath the water one more time.

When Naaman dipped that seventh time, he brought his faith and, with it, his obedience and his humility to the seventh level, and all of a sudden the supernatural broke through. He had insisted on doing it *"according to the saying of the man of God,"* and it worked.

Why was Naaman healed? Because he submitted to the will of God for his life. Because he humbled himself and agreed to do things God's way. Because he agreed to follow God's order of things. Fives times was not enough, and six was not either. It had to be seven. And seven it was. Then the miracle came.

Seven is the stamp or seal of the work of God. All though the Bible this number is a symbol of God's covenant with Israel and their land, and everything pertaining to that land was blessed as long as God's people remained in His order.

Naaman was not an Israelite, but it worked for him too. The moment he completed the seventh dip, his healing was completed.

Before that, there had been Nothing. Now he was whole, and a new life opened up before him.

What's this story all about? This is a process, a humbling process, a faith-building and faith-maintaining process, a process of obedience and a process of enduring. You can finish well, but not if you give up before you reach the seventh level and not if you allow pride to hinder you.

Naaman probably could never have imagined what would actually be required of him, and when he was told, it didn't seem reasonable, but it worked. His skin was renewed like that of a baby. It was brand new and beautiful.

I don't know how old Naaman might have been at the time, but he was probably not a young man to have reached such a lofty position. At whatever age, when he got home I'm sure everyone was asking him what special cream he had used on his journey. He looked absolutely wonderful. God's order brings wonderful healings.

So what are you waiting for? Press on to *The Seventh Level.*

Chapter 13

# The Testing of God's Word in You

*The words of the Lord are pure words; as silver tried in a furnace of earth purified seven times.*

Psalm 12:6

God desires that His Word in you be put to the test. He loves it when His Word is tested and prevails. That makes Him look good.

Of course, it doesn't change God when you fail the test. His Word is still pure and powerful. It just needs to be more pure and powerful in you and through you.

God never changes, and His Word never changes — regardless. But He loves it when you pass the test, showing that His Word is being refined in you. He will allow the tests to keep coming until they have affected you and His Word is so perfectly pure within you that you, too, are purified and sanctified. This will happen as you not only allow and permit, but also welcome His Word to be tested within you to the highest degree.

It's one thing to hear the Word preached, say "amen," and then tell the preacher how good it was, but it's another thing entirely when that word you just heard and dared to say amen to is allowed to be tested in you, and tested, and tested some more, until that test has reached the highest level.

When the Word of the Lord is tested within you, you go through it personally. You experience it mentally, emotionally, and physically. It might even affect your marriage and your finances. Whatever the case, God desires that the process of this refining be completed, that it go all the way to the determined end. He desires that your faith be brought to that seventh level.

Why, some might ask, would the Word of the Lord need to be tried at all? And why would it need to be tried to this level? We know that the words or sayings of the Lord are pure. But it must be tried because it is brought forth by human vessels, and then it is executed by human vessels. When the word of the Lord comes forth to us, it must be without the mixture of falsehoods. Then, once it is hidden in our hearts, we must be careful with our thoughts, our traditions, and our established doctrines.

These days we have a host of input sources that all feed into us. Consider your favorite television and radio preachers, convention speakers, authors, and foreign visitors. Each of these has a part in what resides in your soul. It has always been important to *"rightly divide the word of truth"* (2 Timothy 2:15), and it is even more important today. This is the responsibility, not only of every minister of the Gospel, but also of every Christian believer. Truth sets us free; mixtures do not.

So the problem is not with God and His Word; the problem is with us. He is pure and holy, and His Word is pure and holy. Our world, however, is filled with deceit, and, tragically, that deceit has infiltrated the Church on many levels.

God established the Church for His holy purposes, but today it is being used for many wrong purposes. So, although the Word of God is pure and holy, undefiled, and free from all human mixtures, and, therefore, free from fraud and deceit, not all preaching is all that pure, and not every aspect of your own thinking is necessarily free from error.

The apostle Paul, in writing to the Corinthians, presented *"the promises of God"* as being *"yea"* and *"amen"*:

> *For all the promises of God in him are yea, and in him Amen, unto the glory of God by us.*
>
> 2 Corinthians 1:20

The failure is never in the Scriptures. They are truth, *"yea"* and *"amen"* in Christ Jesus.

Since there is no corruption in the character of God, there is no corruption in His Word. Everything He says lines up with the purity of His nature and character. That is why we can affirm, without a doubt, that the words of the Lord are pure. They are pure because He is pure. They are love because He is love. They are powerful because He is powerful.

Many passages of the Bible confirm the purity of the Word of God. This is especially prominent in the Psalms:

> *Thy word is very pure; therefore thy servant loveth it.* Psalm 119:140

Can you say, from the bottom of your heart, that you love God's Word because you have found it to be pure. You can't say it if you haven't first believed it and then been tested on that belief. There is no room here for your personal feelings and opinions. *"The word of the LORD is very pure."* PERIOD!

When God's Word is allowed to work in us, the purity of that Word purifies us. And when we have become purified by that purified Word, then we can truly say, "I love it."

The Word of God is not just pure; it is *"very pure."* This means it is vehemently holy. Wow! Don't mess with God's Word.

When God speaks, His Word can be determined to be so very pure and so very holy (in a vehement way) that He has declared that we cannot defile His Word and get away with it. He will not allow it. He has said that He is pure, His Word is pure, and His ways are pure. His Word is vehemently wholesome. It is exceedingly purified and, therefore, exceedingly clean.

This word *pure* means "refined from all dross or foreign matters, mixtures, and corruptions," and this refers to the absence of the elements of the doctrines of men. This is our problem.

We have so many different Christian denominations in the world today, many of which we may never have heard of, and in these many different denominations of churches, we have so many preachers cropping up. Some of these new preachers, it seems, have no respect for basic Christian foundations nor for the established fivefold ministry and what it represents. They have no respect for established ministries or established ministers, and they teach and practice disrespect for those who are founded on the Rock of Christ Jesus. This is poisoning our emerging generations.

The Word of God is *"very pure,"* and, as such, it is free from the influence of new-age and humanistic teachings. These two powerful forces have made their way into the twenty-first century church, but they are not based upon the purity of the Word of God.

In the days of the early church, God's power was so at work in the men and women who loved Him that Paul described it like this:

> *But if all prophesy, and there come in one that believeth not, or one unlearned, he is convinced of all, he is judged of all: and thus are the secrets of his heart made manifest; and so falling down on his face he will worship God, and report that God is in you of a truth.* 1 Corinthians 14:24-25

That's how the purity of the words of God works, and it is not happening much in most of our newer churches. What is being taught there is very different.

But God makes it very clear to us that we cannot change His Word. It is what it is, and it will not change for any man. In many modern churches, not only are men not hearing the pure Word of God, but that pure Word is also not being tested in them.

Why do I say this? Many modern Christians hate anything that sounds like a test or trial, and so they stay far from it. They refuse to accept that God means what He says, and so the pure Word of God is not finding a place in their hearts. The result is that it cannot be tested in them. I'm afraid that many pastors will have to answer to God on the Day of Judgment for their failure in this regard. In attempting to make the Christian life easy so that more people will join them, they have robbed people of their true destinies.

The psalmist declared that he was not afraid of the Word of God or its workings in him. He loved it because he knew it to be exceedingly perfect, fully purified. In this case, what we love will be tested and tested again. It will be tested the third time, the fifth time, and the seventh time ... until what has become so pure will make us pure as well.

Do you love the Word of God? Have you hidden it in your heart? If you answer yes, then you must be ready for that word to be proved in you. You may be on level two now. If so, get ready for more testing. God will surely take that word that has been in your spirit and test you on it, to see if you really love it.

When tests suddenly come at you from every side, relax and know that God is working in you to test His Word in you. What He has spoken to you from the Scriptures in preaching and through the prophetic word must be tested and proven real.

Sometimes it seems to us that God is much too harsh, or even that He is rather mean because of what He allows to come to us. Is this true? Is God mean? No, not at all! The fact that He allows serious tests to come to us just indicates how very serious He is about this matter. He means business. His Word must be proven within us, and the result is that we are being refined by the proving of that Word. If God's Word is pure and our desire is to be pure, then we must allow Him to test that Word in us until we rise to the necessary level of purity in our lives, our doings and our goings.

This is a struggle, for the enemy will oppose us at every level. He will use people around us to try to inject a mixture of beliefs into our spirits, and if we receive such a mixture, this grieves the Holy Ghost. Too often, when we compromise and allow some mixture to come in, then it comes like an avalanche and overwhelms our faith.

What must we do? Cling to that Word that is *"as silver tried in a furnace of earth purified seven times."* Silver that has been purified seven times through fire is of the purest known quality, and God's Word is as pure as it gets. And just as silver that has been purified in this way is very valuable, the Word of God in us is priceless.

When precious metals are submitted to fire, it is not to destroy or devalue them. Just the opposite is true. It is to bring out their true value. And when you are submitted to the fires of testing, that is also the goal. If you remain faithful through the test, you will emerge a better person, more valuable, of greater worth.

What does it mean to be of greater value or worth in the Kingdom of God? It means that He can entrust you with more. He can give you new ministries. He can elevate and promote you. Why? Because you have been willing to be tried seven times, and you were determined to pass every test and make it to the seventh level.

The Scriptures teach very clearly that when we have been faithful in that which is *"least,"* more responsibility will be given to us:

> *He that is faithful in that which is least is faithful also in much: and he that is unjust in the least is unjust also in much.* Luke 16:10

When we are faithful *"over a few things,"* He will make us *"ruler over many things"*:

> *His lord said unto him, Well done, thou good and faithful servant: thou hast been faithful over a few things, I will make thee ruler over many things: enter thou into the joy of thy lord.*
> Matthew 25:21

The Kingdom is looking for those who can rule, that is manage and minister on greater levels of anointing. Will you be one of those?

Let me emphasize again: when the Scriptures speak of being purified seven times, it is not necessarily an exact number. It just means many times, enough times. Don't misunderstand me and think that you will experience only seven trials in life to prove a word God has placed in your heart. No, He will decide when it's enough. He will know when you have reached the necessary level of purity. He will know when your refinement is complete. Leave the number of test in His capable hands.

Don't despise God's desire that you be completely and perfectly pure. Don't despise the seven-fold trying of His Word in you. Don't limit Him to how many times He can test you or how or when. Leave these decisions with Him. Seven times just means a perfect or complete number of times, and only He is qualified to say when that has been accomplished. Your responsibility is simply to obey, to persevere, to endure to the end, and He will decide when that end is.

Tests come to us in many forms. Some are physical, some are financial, and some involve our marriage, our children, or our grandchildren. Something about the people around you may test you. Something about your job may test you. It might be politics, race, or money that tests the Word of the Lord in you. Whatever comes your way and however it comes, know that God loves you and wants to bring you to the place where you can say, "I love the Word of God because it is pure, and it's working in me is purifying me."

If this is true, people around you will know it. They will see that you love the Word of God, because you live it, it flows out from you, and when it flows out from you, it is so pure that it affects others and changes them too. The perfecting of your faith will touch many other lives.

So in the Scriptures, where it says *"seven times,"* it just means "frequently, very often, again and again," and God has designed it that way. He longs to bring you to the place that He can say, "Faithful one, I have a promotion for you."

Too many of us are waiting around to get promoted, but what we need to do is pass the test that we are currently dealing with. Your future depends on your obedience in the here and now. Stop waiting on the Lord in this respect; waiting around is just hindering your progress.

You need to be concentrating on passing the current test by allowing the Word of the Lord that you have heard to work in you. You need to be faithful and stand on that Word. When you have done that to the level that God requires (and only He can say what that level is), then all of a sudden those blessings and promotions you have been waiting on will emerge. Promotion comes suddenly, but it requires that we fulfill the daily process of testing.

When promotion comes it means that you have been faithful to the process of refining, and it was repeated often enough that the silver in you has become pure.

Another psalm that speaks of the trying of God's Word is the eighteenth:

> *As for God, His way is perfect; the word of the* LORD *is tried ... .* Psalm 18:30

The fact that the Word of God has to be tried takes the excitement out of it for many of us. We want instant gratification. We want it all right here and right now. But there are many factors that affect the outcome.

For one thing, the Word of God must come to us as revealed truth. If it's not revealed truth, we won't love it. If it's not revealed truth, it won't mean anything to us. It is only when it has become revealed truth to us that God will then begin the testing process. That revealed truth is wonderful, but for it to be effective, it must first be brought to the seventh level within us. So the Word of truth in you, even when it is a revealed truth, will be tried and tested.

The Word of truth will be tried in the days ahead by advances in modern science, it will be tried through current literature and the arts, it will be tried through all the "advances" in society and by the immorality of our modern world. It will be tried in and through the courts and through the laws of our land. It will be tried in our President, tried in our Congress, and tried through our state and local governments. And it will be tried in every individual. No one is exempt.

The Word of the Lord is being tried in the face of the Humanism, Atheism, and New-Age philosophies of Hollywood and the many godless celebrities that work there. It is being tried in the face of all enemies of truth everywhere.

Personally I never imagined that the day would come when our politicians, from the highest post in Washington, D.C. to the lowest local level, would be abandoning the Word of God in such large numbers and passing laws so contrary to its teachings. Anything that men and women want to do these days is being deemed acceptable, lawful, and protected behavior. May God help us!

State after state is giving legal sanction to same-sex marriage, and no consideration is being given to what God, the Creator of man and women and the Originator of marriage, has to say about it. And we know that it will only get worse in the days ahead.

More and more blatantly sinful people are being looked upon as experts and spokespeople for all sorts of things, and they are speaking out very boldly for their way of life. Rather than steer our modern generations to a better way, society seems to be falling at the feet of these evil ones. But this doesn't change God or His Word. The Word of God will stand forever.

His Word is still pure, it is *"very pure,"* and I choose to stand upon it and not compromise. He is still at work through His true Church, the virgin Bride of Christ, and He continues to prove Himself through those who love Him and desire for His Kingdom to rule on Earth, even as it does in Heaven.

Contrary to what many are now preaching, trials, tests, temptations, and persecution will all come our way in the days ahead, and this is a normal and necessary part of our spiritual growth. Those who try to make the Christian life look so very easy and who refuse to preach against sin are not sent by God. This is not His teaching.

We are daily faced with a lot of negativity against the true Church in our news media, and until the Church is ready to stand up and be the Church, nothing will change. If we continue to elect godless politicians, what can we expect? As for God, His way is perfect, and the Word of the Lord is tried and found faithful.

If persecution could smother and destroy the Word of God it would have done so decades ago. It won't happen. If ridicule, intellectual arguments, and hatred of the word *holiness* could smother the Word, it would have done so long ago. It can't, and it won't.

Jesus said:

> *Upon this rock I will build my church; and the gates of hell shall not prevail against it.*
>
> Matthew 16:18

They *"shall not prevail."* Period!

Intellectualism will not prevail. Humanism will not prevail. New-Age doctrines will not prevail. God is building a Church, a people, that will not be easily destroyed. His people, those called-out ones, those members of His Body and His Church, will love His Word, and because they trust it and they trust Him, will allow it to be tested and tried in them at every level until victory comes.

They know it as reality, as truth. They know and experience it as the revealed word, and they will stick with it through every test until they emerge as pure gold. This is the Church God desires, and we must determine to be part of it.

Like most of you, I listen to the news and wonder if the people making headlines, running our country, and making our laws ever read the Bible. Do they not know what the book of Romans says? What kinds of parents did our senators and representatives have? It is scary to contemplate what our near future might look like. We must stand firm and be faithful to the teachings of the Word of God.

We cannot compromise, Church, and we must permit or allow the testings of God's Word to work in us to bring us to the seventh level and beyond, that we will live out the revealed truth.

Paul wrote to the Romans:

> *For I am not ashamed of the gospel of Christ: for it is the power of God unto salvation to every one that believeth; to the Jew first, and also to the Greek.*
>
> Romans 1:16

This word *ashamed* indicates that I know it works. How do I know it works? Because I have tried it, and it has tried me. That is why Paul could say that he was not ashamed of the Gospel of Christ.

How did he know that it was *"the power of God unto salvation"*? Because he had tried it, and it had tried him. He knew it worked because it had worked in him.

The psalmist declared:

> *For thou O God hast proved us; thou hast tried us, as silver is tried.* Psalm 66:10

There it is again. This word *prove,* as used here, means that God comes to investigate our spirits. He is looking in there to see what level we are on. It means "to investigate and to examine you by testing you."

The word *tried* in the Scriptures means "to go ahead and give you the test." God will investigate you and examine you. Then He will prep you like they do in the hospital. He will faithfully prep you for the coming tests.

Here are some more powerful passages that confirm His proving nature:

> *Thou hast proved mine heart; thou hast visited me in the night; thou hast tried me, and shalt find nothing; I am purposed that my mouth shall not transgress.*
> Psalm 17:3

*And thou shall remember all the way which the* Lord *thy God led thee these forty years in the wilderness, to humble thee, and to prove thee, to know what was in thine heart, whether thou wouldest keep his commandments, or no.*

Deuteronomy 8:2

Why can't God be easy on us? Because He loves us, and we love Him, and He wants the very best for our lives.

Another such verse follows in quick succession:

*Who fed thee in the wilderness with manna, which thy fathers knew not, that he might humble thee, and that he might prove thee, to do thee good at thy latter end.* Deuteronomy 8:16

Let's get ready for it. Let's get down and humbled before the Lord. He knows how to work these things out and how to prove and test us so that we can do good things in His Kingdom in the last days.

If you can't make it now, the way things currently stand, you are in trouble, because it will definitely get worse (see 2 Timothy 3:13).

Moses wrote:

*Thou shalt not hearken unto the words of that prophet, or that dreamer of dreams; for the* Lord *your God proveth you, to know whether ye love the*

> *LORD your God with all your heart and with all your soul.* Deuteronomy 13:3

There are a lot of false prophets in our land. Sometimes you allow them to place their hands on you, and to speak into your life, even though you don't really know them or know them well. This is a dangerous practice.

I am determined to know those who labor among us (see 1 Thessalonians 5:12), and I am determined not to allow any man to lay hands on me suddenly (see 1 Timothy 5:22). We have all failed in these areas and need to do better.

I try to be very careful about who I bring in to minister to our church. For me to invite someone, they have to have a proven ministry. I want to know them, and if I don't know them, I find out about them. I don't want just any preacher coming to preach to our people, laying hands on them and prophesying. I am determined to know who is false and who is real.

Proverbs speaks of the Lord's work of trying us:

> *The fining pot is for silver, and the furnace for gold; but the LORD trieth the hearts.*
>
> Proverbs 17:3

God will try us, and that is hard, but He will also grace you so that you can survive every test.

## The Testing of God's Word in You

The Scriptures clearly show that the Lord tries the heart, and He does it in many different ways:

> *Behold, I have refined thee, but not with silver; I have chosen thee in the furnace of affliction.* Isaiah 48:10

> *Wherein ye greatly rejoice, though now for a season, if need be, ye are in heaviness through manifold temptations. That the trial of your faith, being much more precious than of gold that perisheth, though it be tried with fire, might be found unto praise and honour and glory at the appearing of Jesus Christ.*
> 1 Peter 1:6-7

When the Lord next comes to visit you in your bedroom, will it be to His glory and honor? When the door is closed and you are dealing with your hurts, and with His various tryings and testings, and suddenly He comes through the door, will you be found faithful?

Let us say, "Lord, I accept Your will. I accept Your Word in me, and therefore I accept the tests that come to prove that Word. And I will be faithful."

Let Him bring you from level to level to level, and don't stop the process of the workings of God. He will work in your circumstances and gain from it all the praise and honor.

So what are you waiting for? Press today toward *The Seventh Level.*

## Chapter 14

# Dad's Great Example

*Who his own self bare our sins in his own body on the tree, that we, being dead to sins, should live unto righteousness: by whose stripes ye were healed.*

1 Peter 2:24

I was born and raised in a Christian home, one of eleven children, and we attended a wonderful Spirit-filled church. My father, Milton C. Blount, was a man of prayer and of great faith, and he taught me much, both by his words and by his holy example.

In 1954, when I was eight, Dad became very ill. This went on for weeks and grew progressively worse, so that he knew something was seriously wrong in his abdominal area. In those days people didn't go to doctors much, especially people of faith. They preferred to let God heal them.

One day Dad decided to go to a doctor and be diagnosed, but he had no intention of undergoing surgery. He wanted to have his condition officially recorded on paper so that when he was healed (and he was sure that he *would* be), everyone could know what God had done. He relished the idea of the doctor himself seeing this great miracle.

Several days after his visit to Dr. Reed, the doctor called to give him the bad news. He had a bleeding malignant tumor the size of a grapefruit. He would require surgery, and the doctor had taken the liberty of scheduling it.

But Dad was on a journey of faith. He believed that his sickness was just a trial of that faith, and he had declared to our mom and to the older children that he was going to trust God for his healing. He was sure that he would be healed, and nothing could dissuade him now. He continued to hold out for that healing.

Weeks went by and his condition grew worse. He became increasingly weak and suffered terribly from pain. He was unable to eat much, so his weight began dropping precipitously.

Dr. Reed called again and asked, "Mr. Blount, why are you not going to be operated on?"

Dad replied, "My Jesus is going to heal me."

Dr. Reed said, "I'm sorry, Mr. Blount, but Jesus is *not* going to heal you. He has left that for me to do."

Dad didn't see it that way. Not long after that, he had a vision one day. He was in his bedroom, where he now spent the most of his time, and suddenly the ceiling, the walls and the furniture faded out, and another scene came before him.

He saw himself lying on an operating table. He said it was so real that he could have reached out and touched himself. Dr. Reed was there, with another doctor and two nurses, and they were standing around him. Dr. Reed proceeded to cut him open. Then, when he had looked inside, he shook his head and proceeded to sew Dad back up again. When he was finished, Dad was wheeled out of the operating room, and the vision faded.

As the bedroom came back into view, Dad knew that he was being sent home to die, and he knew that he had made the right decision about having surgery. In that moment, God spoke to him in a loud voice and said, "Trust in man, and you shall die. Trust in Me, and you shall live." That strengthened Dad's faith and determination. Still, day-by-day and week-by-week, he continued to get worse.

I was just a small boy, but I remember sitting by Dad's bed and hearing him pray. He would speak in the Spirit in the most beautiful languages, and then God would give him the interpretation of those words. I can still hear him saying: "Only believe! The same God who filled you with the Holy Ghost shall heal you in due season." In this way, God encouraged Dad many times.

Now Dad became so weak that he had times of unconsciousness and seemed to leave us for hours. The tumor in his side began to hemorrhage, and Mom had difficulty keeping up with the bleeding. At one point, she wrapped sheets around him to catch the blood. He was a large robust man with a reddish complexion, but now he became as white as the sheets that enveloped him. Still, Dad held to his faith, rising to a new level of determination.

The pastor of our church would come to pray for Dad and would bring with him his family members and other believers who could pray, but he was not as certain of victory as Dad was. "Please go get operated on," he urged Dad. "You have your wife and these eleven children to consider."

Dad's answer was always the same, "My Jesus is going to heal me."

One day I was kneeling at Dad's bedside while he was unconscious. My head was level with his. He suddenly came to and when he did, he reached for a nearby yellow pencil and note pad and began to write slowly on it. His note was addressed to my mother. "Corilea," it said, "when I get so bad, don't let them take me to the hospital. My Jesus is going to heal me." Mom assured him that she stood with his decision of faith to trust God fully, and she would honor his request. Still, he got worse.

Many days of pain and weakness followed (and there were no available pain medications in those days). All that Dad had to comfort him were the promises of God. He clung to Isaiah 53:5 and 1 Peter 2:24:

> *But he was wounded for our transgressions, he was bruised for our iniquities: the chastisement of our peace was upon him; and with his stripes we are healed.* Isaiah 53:5

> *Who his own self bare our sins in his own body on the tree, that we, being dead to sins, should live unto righteousness: by whose stripes ye were healed.* 1 Peter 2:24

As each new physical challenge came, Dad seemed to rise to a new level of faith to face it. He was determined. He would be healed. God had promised it, and God can't fail.

One morning, after he had come to from a period of unconsciousness, Dad was meditating on the woman of Mark 5:

> *And a certain woman, which had an issue of blood twelve years, and had suffered many things of many physicians, and had spent all that she had, and was nothing bettered, but rather grew worse, when she had heard of Jesus, came in the press behind, and touched his garment. For she said, If I may touch but his clothes, I shall be whole.* Mark 5:25-28

In Dad's words, here's what happened next:

"Suddenly there was the most beautiful and brightest light that flashed into my bedroom. A power surge went through my whole body, and a cool feeling went into my left side. I knew that I was instantly healed. I knew that I had received a blood transfusion.

"I began to touch my side. Then I began to press on my side. Before this, I couldn't stand for a sheet to touch my side; the pain was so bad.

"Now I started shouting to my wife, who was in the kitchen, 'Sugar, Sugar, come here. Jesus has healed me.'

"She ran to the bedroom and found me beating my left side and shouting, 'Jesus has healed me.' And I've been healed ever since."

Dad lived for another fifty years and never tired of telling this story ... until God finally took him home at a ripe old age. I could not finish this book without telling you the story, because, you see, this is where I got my first inspiration to hold on to faith and rise from level to level with each new challenge life sends our way … until victory comes at last. It must come, for God has promised.

So, what about you, my friend? Will your faith rise to *The Seventh Level?*

# *Ministry Page*

You may contact Pastor Lloyd Blount in any of the following ways.


Lloyd Blount<br>
P.O. Box 1742<br>
Hammond, LA 70404

rablount@bellsouth.net

www.alchammond.org

# Crossing Your Jordans

The Now. The New. The Next.

REGINA BLOUNT

www.ingramcontent.com/pod-product-compliance
Lightning Source LLC
LaVergne TN
LVHW011328080426
835513LV00006B/250